THE
WHITE HOLE
IN TIME

THE
WHITE HOLE
IN TIME

Our Future Evolution and the Meaning of Now

PETER RUSSELL

HarperSanFrancisco
A Division of HarperCollins*Publishers*

Harper San Francisco and the author, in association with the
Rainforest Action Network, will facilitate the planting of two
trees for every one tree used in the manufacture of this book.

FIRST EDITION
SIMULTANEOUSLY PUBLISHED BY THE AQUARIAN PRESS, LONDON.

Library of Congress Cataloging-in-Publication Data
Russell, Peter.
    The white hole in time : our future evolution and the
meaning of now / Peter Russell. — 1st ed.
       p.   cm.
    Includes index.
    ISBN 0–06–250774–5 (alk. paper)
    1. Life.   2. Evolution.   I. Title.
BD431.R77   1992
110—dc20   91–58162
                                     CIP

92 93 94 95 96 AP 10 9 8 7 6 5 4 3 2 1

CONTENTS

RETURN TO NOW

FROM NOW TO ETERNITY

Time is what keeps the light from reaching us.

Meister Eckhart

PREFACE

May you live in interesting times.

Old Chinese Curse

Have you ever gazed up at the stars on a clear night and wondered what it's all about? What's going on out there in the vastness of space? And what are we doing here on Earth? Is life very rare, if not unique, in the Universe? Or are we human beings utterly insignificant?

In terms of physical size and location we certainly are of little significance. In the words of *The Hitchhiker's Guide to the Galaxy*, 'Space is big . . . vastly hugely mindbogglingly big . . .' Every star that you see is a star in our own galaxy. And for every one of these there are thousands more far too faint to be seen with the naked eye. It may be hard to imagine, but our own galaxy contains many billions of stars. And as if this were not enough to dwarf us completely, this galaxy is but one of a billion other unseen galaxies.

We are also of little import in terms of time. If the Universe's billions of years were compressed into the span of one human lifetime, our own existence would occupy only a second. As ancient Indian texts put it, 'We are but a wink in the eye of Brahman.'

In this context humanity certainly does not seem significant. But I hope to show you that something is happening on this planet that is very significant indeed. We could be standing on the threshold of a moment towards which the Universe has been building since time began – an evolutionary climax more profound than any of us could dare to imagine.

Stated so bluntly that may sound like science fiction. I prefer to think of it as science faction – a portrayal of our possible destiny based on currently accepted theories and ideas.

A Tapestry of Ideas

This book is not about one single theme. It is a tapestry of ideas; a picture of many colors, drawing upon many areas – physics, biology, philosophy, religion, psychology, and personal experience, to name but some. Not all of the ideas will be new to you. What *is* new is the picture that forms as the various themes weave together. Then the familiar becomes fascinating, and a new vision emerges of ourselves and our place in the Universe.

In building on the contemporary scientific understanding of the world, I do not wish to imply that this worldview is necessarily correct. Perhaps the only eternal truth of science is that all theories change with time. What I am interested in are the broader implications of our as-yet imperfect understanding of the world. What is it pointing towards? Where does it suggest our species may be heading?

Overview

The first part of the book, 'From Nowhere to Now,' sets the scene. It presents an overview of the major leaps in biological evolution that have led to humanity, and the major leaps in cultural evolution that have brought us to the present day. It asks: What are the factors that have made human beings one of the most remarkable creatures ever to have lived on this planet – not only in terms of the changes we have created, but also in terms of the potentials inherent in our self-consciousness?

The second part, 'Now but Not Now,' is more analytical – and initially more gloomy. It starts by exploring the less wholesome sides of humanity's rapid development, and the devastation we are bringing to the rest of the planet. How is it, we ask, that a species in some ways so intelligent can in other ways be so stupid? Where have we gone wrong? Why are we so self-centered?

These questions lead on to an exploration of our inner needs and the way that our societies have seduced us – in effect hypnotized us – into a set of false assumptions. We see how the global crisis is, at its root, a crisis of perception and thinking – a crisis of consciousness.

If we are to navigate ourselves safely through this moment of history we must make a break with the past, and look at ourselves and our world with fresh eyes. This will entail a fundamental shift in thinking and perception – a shift in consciousness more profound than any in our history. Could this be the next step in our collective evolution?

'Return to Now' is more spiritual in tone. It asks: How can we dehypnotize ourselves? How can we liberate our thinking and make the inner changes that are being demanded of us?

This part considers the nature of that most intimate aspect of our existence, our sense of 'I.' Because we usually identify with our sensory experience of the world, we err in thinking that we exist solely in time and space. But some simple thought experiments show that the self is, in some senses, beyond both time and space. Much as it may contradict our day-to-day experience we are, at our core, timeless beings.

Some little-explored implications of Einstein's Special Theory of Relativity reveal the fascinating possibility that the same is true for light as for consciousness. Here, too, time and timelessness coexist. The 'now' of light, it turns out, has the same characteristics as the 'now' of our experience. Could there be some deeper relationship between the two? What else do light and consciousness have in common?

The final part, 'From Now to Eternity,' looks to the future. It considers some of the many prophecies that seem to foretell these turbulent times. And it looks behind their literal interpretations to deeper meanings, suggesting that they are metaphors for inner transformation and awakening.

Will we wake up in time, and so avoid catastrophe? That is a very open question. If we do not, evolution on this planet could be kicked back to a new Dark Age perhaps; or worse, back to the primeval soup. On the other hand, if we do come to our senses, then it seems very likely that our rate of development – particularly our rate of inner development – will continue to grow faster and faster. What will happen if change is compressed from decades to years to months . . .? Could it be that, just as matter is drawn into a black hole in space, the destiny of human evolution may be a 'white hole in time' – a moment of unimaginably rapid transformation.

Finally we ask whether there could after all be a purpose to evolution. Surprisingly, perhaps, a recent cosmological hypothesis suggests that there is. The Universe seems to be set up so that conscious creatures like us can evolve, capable of knowing Creation in all its dimensions. Could we be the species that completes this process of cosmic self-discovery here on planet Earth?

Bon Voyage

Touching as it does on many themes, a lot has been packed into the pages of this book. The material in any one chapter could easily be expanded into a book of its own. But rather than pad the material with examples, I have tried to explain each point briefly and clearly, fit it into the larger picture, and then move on to explore another piece of this cosmic jigsaw.

Naturally I have tried to make it an easy read – what writer doesn't? But it is still a read that requires your participation. Some of the material contains implications that I only touch on, or occasionally merely hint at. There may be many points where you want to pause and digest, or perhaps explore the ramifications for your own picture of the world. In short, it is a book to meditate upon as much as simply read.

It need hardly be said that the picture painted in these pages is only one of many possible pictures. You may well want to weave the threads together in a different way. Please do. My aim is not to prove a theory. It is to explore possibilities that we may not have considered, and to see where they lead. I want to raise questions more than give answers.

Above all, I hope you receive as much inspiration from the reading as I did from the writing. And as much enjoyment.

December 1, 1990,
Los Angeles

FROM NOWHERE TO NOW

As once the winged energy of delight
carried you over childhood's dark abysses,
now beyond your own life build the great
arch of unimagined bridges.

Wonders happen if we can succeed
in passing through the harshest danger;
but only in a bright and purely granted
achievement can we realize the wonder.

To work with Things in the indescribable
relationship is not too hard for us;
the pattern grows more intricate and subtle,
and being swept along is not enough.

Take your practiced powers and stretch them out
until they span the chasm between two
contradictions . . . For the god
wants to know himself in you.

Rainer Maria Rilke

ACCELERATION – THE PACE OF LIFE

... these most brisk and giddy-paced times.

William Shakespeare

'The pace of life is speeding up.' Hardly the most startling statement. As most of us are only too aware, change comes more and more rapidly. Technological breakthroughs spread through society in years rather than centuries. Calculations that would have taken decades are now made in minutes. Communication that used to take months happens in seconds. Development in almost all areas is happening faster and faster.

As a result more and more of us are living in the fast lane – many in overdrive. There is more information to absorb, more challenges to meet, more skills to learn, more tasks to accomplish. Yet the time to fit it all in seems to be getting less and less. 'Acceleration syndrome' has become an intimate part of our lives.

Worse still, there is no sign that things are getting any better. On the contrary, the pace of life will probably get faster and faster, taking us deeper and deeper into what Alvin Toffler called 'Future Shock . . . the shattering stress and disorientation that we induce in individuals by subjecting them to too much change in too short a time.'

Will we be able to cope? This, argued Toffler, is the challenge facing us. To learn to handle ever-more rapid change without burning out or breaking down.

It is not only humanity that is under stress. Our accelerating pace of change is putting increasing pressure on the planet. There are ever-growing numbers of us to feed, clothe, and house. Our waste is pouring into the air, the soil, and the seas many times faster than our environment can absorb it. Seldom in its history has the Earth changed so rapidly.

And the faster the world around us changes, the more we are forced to let go of any cozy notions we might have of what the future will be like. No one today can predict with any degree of certainty how things will be in one year's time, or even six months' time. When global stockmarkets can crash without warning, political walls crumble overnight, countries invade each other in a day, and ecological disasters shatter our illusions of control, we are forced more and more to live in the present.

To live with continued acceleration and all it brings will take more than simply learning to manage better. As we shall see, we must change our attitudes to time itself. This will involve a complete revision of our thinking about who we are, what we really want, what our lives are all about — and what Life itself is all about.

An Eternal Trend

Looking back over history it is clear that acceleration is not just a twentieth-century phenomenon. Change occurs much faster today than it did a thousand years ago — medieval architecture and agriculture, for instance, varied very little over the period of a century. But even then change occurred much faster than it did in prehistoric times — Stone Age tools remained unchanged for thousands of years.

Not only is this gathering of pace a feature of human civilization, it is a pattern that stretches back through the history of life on Earth. According to currently accepted theories — and it is well worth remembering that most scientific theories change with time — human beings first appeared on Earth about a quarter-million years ago. Mammals started evolving much earlier, about 60 million years ago. And the first living cells appeared even earlier still — some 3,500 million years ago.

Nor did the trend begin there. Before any living system could evolve other equally important developments had to occur. This too was an evolutionary process that accelerated.

Evolution in Perspective

Most cosmologists now believe that the Universe started between 10,000 million and 20,000 million years ago as an 11-dimensional Universe of pure energy – unimaginably hot and extremely compact. Seven of the dimensions 'collapsed' in upon themselves, becoming what we observe as the fundamental forces of nature – gravity, electromagnetism, and the weak and strong nuclear forces. The four remaining dimensions we know as the three of space and the one of time.

Intense internal pressures caused this four-dimensional Universe to expand very rapidly – creating the so-called 'Big Bang.' As the Universe expanded it cooled and condensed into elementary particles – electrons, positrons, photons, and neutrinos. Cooling further, these particles began forming stable relationships with each other and so gave birth to the very simplest of atoms: hydrogen and helium.

Matter had been born.

It took millions of years, however, for more complex atoms to form. This could only happen when simpler atoms chanced to collide and combine. Over many eons this fusion process created all the elements lighter than iron. But here the chain stopped.

The synthesis of heavier elements (e.g. cobalt, nickel, copper, gold, uranium) requires the input of additional energy. This could not happen for several billion years, until the lighter elements had formed stars, and these stars had themselves become 'supernova' – the massive thermonuclear furnaces created when stars collapse in upon themselves. From the supernova that preceded our own Sun came most of the heavier elements we now find on planet Earth – and in every cell of our bodies.

Matter had evolved, but it had taken ten billion years to create just over a hundred different elements.

This chemical diversity became the foundation-stone for living systems. Once they had become established, the rate of development speeded up. Changes took place not over billions of years, but over millions, and later even faster.

Such lengthy time-scales are so far from our everyday experience that it is hard to appreciate just how rapidly evolution has been gaining speed. To get a better feel for these changes, let us chart the evolution of life against a more familiar visual image – New York's tallest building, the quarter-mile-high World Trade Center.

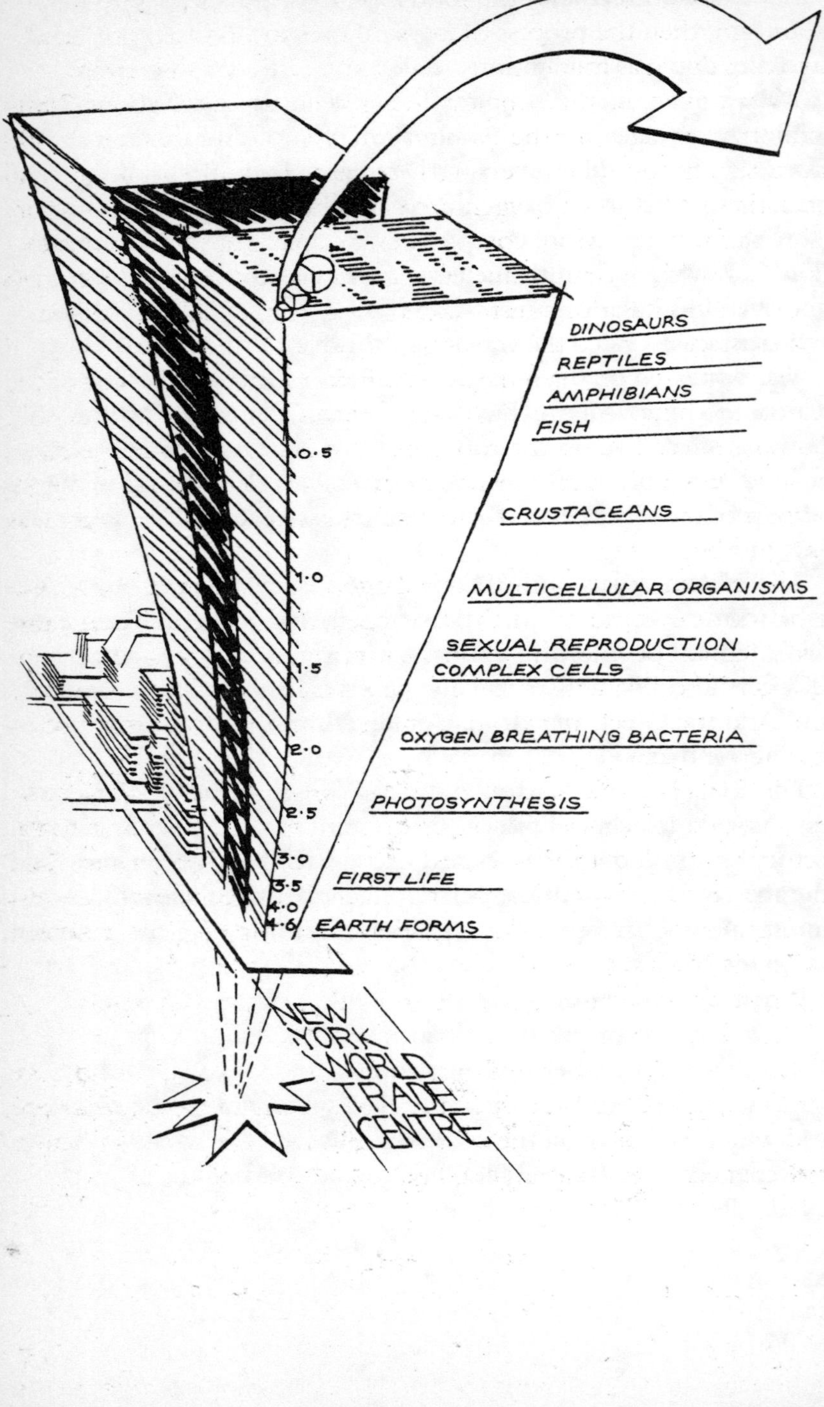

DINOSAURS
REPTILES
AMPHIBIANS
FISH

0·5

CRUSTACEANS

1·0

MULTICELLULAR ORGANISMS

1·5   SEXUAL REPRODUCTION
COMPLEX CELLS

2·0   OXYGEN BREATHING BACTERIA

2·5   PHOTOSYNTHESIS

3·0
3·5   FIRST LIFE
4·0
4·6   EARTH FORMS

NEW YORK WORLD TRADE CENTRE

If we make street level the formation of our planet 4,600 million years ago, then the process of physical evolution which preceded it stretches down as foundations some two-thirds of a mile deep.

Above ground, the simplest living cells appeared about 3,500 million years ago, on the twenty-fifth floor of the building's 108 storeys. Photosynthesis evolved around the fiftieth floor, and bacteria that breathed oxygen came another ten floors later – more than half way up. More complex cells, capable of sexual reproduction and with a central nucleus, appeared around the seventieth floor. Multicellular organisms came another ten floors above that – and crustaceans ruled the waves on the ninety-fourth floor.

Fish appeared on the ninety-seventh floor, and crawled out of the sea on the ninety-ninth. Dinosaurs reigned on floors 104 to 107. And mammals live on the top floor. But *Homo erectus* first walked on two legs only a few inches from the top. It had taken 99.99 percent of life's journey so far to reach this step – and humanity was only just beginning.

The Neanderthals with their enlarged brains, simple tools, and tribal culture appeared in the last quarter of an inch. Then came Cro-Magnon people with clothes, painting, language, and perhaps religion. The Pharaohs ruled Egypt a fiftieth of an inch from the top. And the Greek and Roman empires thrived a hundredth of an inch above that.

The Renaissance occurred in the top one-thousandth of an inch: less than the thickness of a layer of paint. The whole of modern history occupies but the thickness of a microscopic bacterium. And the age of the microchip, rock'n'roll, global telecommunications, nuclear power, moon-walks, and global warming is a layer almost too thin to measure.

Wherever we are going, we are going there faster and faster.

But where are we going?

Before we can answer this question we must first look at how we got to where we are. Why it is that evolution as a whole speeds up? And why it is that of all the creatures on this planet, human beings have created so much change so fast?

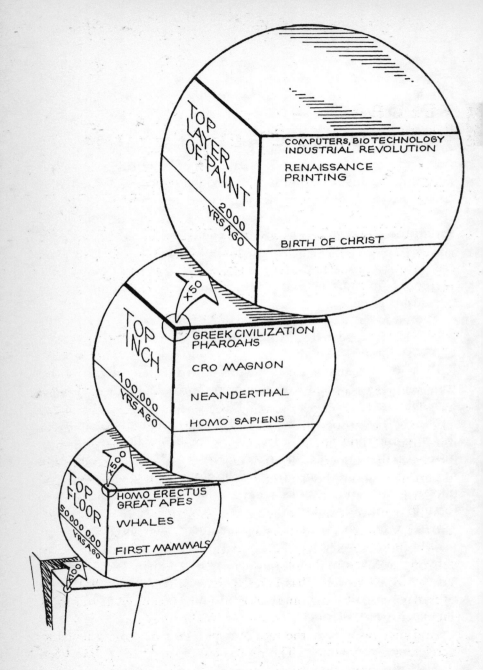

FEEDBACK –
PLATFORMS OF EVOLUTION

The nature of the Universe loves nothing so much as to change things which are and to make new things like them. For everything that exists is in a manner the seed of that which will be.

Marcus Aurelius

What do we mean when we say the rate of evolution has speeded up? The world of physics has not speeded up. As far as we know electrons spin around the nucleus of an atom at the same rate as they did 10,000 million years ago. Nor have the biological processes that underlie evolution changed; they are probably still occurring at about the same rate as they did when life first emerged on Earth.

What has accelerated is the rate at which change has occurred: the rate at which new species have come into being, and the rate at which those species have evolved new characteristics. It is, to borrow a term from the philosopher Alfred North Whitehead, the rate at which 'novelty' has entered the world: novelty, not in its everyday sense of some unusual or curious circumstance, but in its literal sense of 'newness.'

And the reason why the rate of appearance of novelty tends to accelerate is very simple. The more new capacities that have been created, the more opportunity there is for the creation of further new capacities. It is a basic law of life. Creativity breeds creativity.

Systems theorists call this phenomenon 'positive feedback.' One example of positive feedback with which we are all familiar is the growth of population. The more people there are, the more children are born. The more children that are born, the more parents there will be in the future. And so, if there are no constraints, the population grows – and faster and faster.

Another common example of the current state of affairs accelerating future rates of growth is money invested at compound interest. A dollar invested at 10 percent interest would be 'worth' $1.10 after one year; $1.21 after two years; $2.59 after ten years; $117.39 after fifty years; $13,780.65 after a hundred years; and around $2,473,000,000,000,000,000,000,000,000,000,000,000,000, 000,000,000,000,000 after a thousand years. And economists still think it's a good idea! But that's another story.

A Platform for Life

The growth curve of evolution may not have been as smooth or as mathematically precise as the growth of compound interest – the current view is that it has progressed through a series of dramatic fits and starts – but positive feedback has nevertheless been at work, accelerating the overall rate of evolution.

The first molecules were simple compounds composed of just a few atoms. As physical evolution progressed, these collected together into larger, more complex compounds. The more compounds that were created, the greater the possibilities for further combinations – and the more rapidly new molecules appeared.

Through this process there emerged the highly complex macro-molecules of RNA and DNA containing millions of atoms. These brought with them a new and most significant characteristic – they could produce copies of themselves. Nature no longer had to build these macro-molecules through the combination of smaller sub-units; instead each molecule served as a template upon which copies of itself could be built. And these copies served as templates for further copies. All they needed were the right conditions in which to multiply.

It was this development that provided the platform upon which life could emerge and begin to build. Encoded in the structure of these molecules are sets of instructions that, when activated, build up long sequences of amino acids – the basic building blocks of life. The code itself consists of only four 'letters,' but combined in triplets, they form a language of sixty-four words, defining various amino acids. Strung together these words build 'sentences,' often hundreds of words long, defining complex biological molecules. So efficient is this information coding that if the sequence of 'letters' in just one DNA molecule were typed out on paper it would fill a book of 6000 pages.

But DNA is more than just an elegant molecular language. Being able to produce faithful copies also meant that any changes that occurred in the structure of a molecule were automatically passed on. Nature had invented its own way of learning. DNA became life's data bank.

'Remembering' modifications from previous generations, living cells were able to 'learn' those characteristics that enhanced their chances of survival. And the better they survived the faster their numbers grew. In just one billion years of biological evolution a far greater degree of novelty emerged upon this planet than had appeared over the previous ten billion years of stellar evolution. In this comparatively short time life progressed from simple algae and bacteria to complex cells capable of photosynthesis and respiration.

The Leap of Sex

Many of the new characteristics that evolved served as platforms for further developments. A good and oft-cited example is the advent of sexual reproduction some 1,500 million years ago. Until that time cells reproduced by simply splitting into two, each of the new 'sisters' being exact clones of the original. The opportunities for beneficial variation were very small, and any that did occur remained isolated to the descendants of that particular cell.

With sexual reproduction, however, two cells came together, shared their inherited genetic information and produced offspring that contained a combination of their genes. No longer did it take thousands of generations for just one genetic difference to arise. Differences now occurred in every generation.

Moreover, beneficial genetic changes were not limited to a particular clonal line. They could spread rapidly through a population. The result was a dramatic leap in the rate of emergence of new types of cells.

Cellular Cooperation

Multicellular organisms, the first of which appeared some 1,400 million years ago, were another great step for evolution. Working together in a community, it became more efficient for individual cells to take on special functions. Some took on tasks such as digestion, some formed a protective casing, others helped in movement. The added adaptability and stability that this brought helped organisms survive much greater variations in their environment.

From then on evolution was not limited to the creation of new species of cells. The way these cells were organized, the organs they created and the functions they took on became a new platform for evolution. The result was another speeding up of development. The awe-inspiring diversity of species that we see on Earth today evolved in just the last tenth of Earth's history.

From Senses to Brains

As time went on, some organs evolved a new and special function. In addition to processing energy and matter, they could process information. Some developed into senses capable of detecting changes in the environment, others became rudimentary nervous systems able to carry information from one part of the organism to another, and store it for later use. The well-being and survival of these creatures now depended not only on the genetic learning of their ancestors, but also on the learning accumulated during their own lifetimes. And again the rate of change accelerated.

Nervous systems are delicate structures, and the earliest ones, distributed throughout the organism, were very vulnerable. With the evolution of a spinal cord and skull, however, the nervous system was protected inside a case of bone. Once this step had been accomplished the development of the nervous system itself became the major focus of evolution.

We tend to see vertebrate evolution in terms of the more visible changes in outer form – gills evolving into lungs, fins developing into arms and legs – but the most significant changes were taking place on the inside. The nervous system was steadily expanding in size and growing in complexity. The nervous systems of early worms occupied less than one ten-thousandth of the organism. The

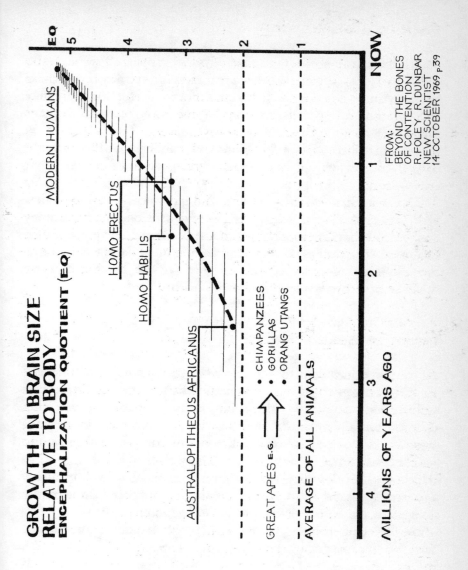

GROWTH IN BRAIN SIZE RELATIVE TO BODY
ENCEPHALIZATION QUOTIENT (EQ)

MODERN HUMANS

HOMO ERECTUS

HOMO HABILIS

AUSTRALOPITHECUS AFRICANUS

GREAT APES E.G.
- CHIMPANZEES
- GORILLAS
- ORANG UTANGS

AVERAGE OF ALL ANIMALS

MILLIONS OF YEARS AGO

NOW

EQ
5
4
3
2
1

FROM:
BEYOND THE BONES
OF CONTENTION
R.FOLEY R.DUNBAR
NEW SCIENTIST
14 OCTOBER 1969 p.39

brain-to-body ratio of *stenonychosaurus,* one of the most intelligent dinosaurs, was probably about twenty times greater, but still not that impressive. With the advent of mammals, however, the nervous system began to grow very rapidly. Within the last 50 million years – less than one third of the dinosaurs' total reign, and only a hundredth of Earth's history – there has been an unprecedented growth in brain size.

We can get an idea of how dramatic this growth has been by considering changes in the 'encephalization quotient' (EQ), which is a measure of the size of an organism's brain relative to its body. The average brain-to-body ratio of all animals is given an EQ value of 1. This serves as a baseline against which the observed brain-to-body ratio of a particular organism can be plotted. The great apes (chimpanzees, gorillas, and orangutans) have an EQ of between 1 and 2. The earliest known hominids had an EQ of just over 2. *Homo habilis,* the first tool-using hominid, had an EQ of over 3, as also did *Homo erectus.* Modern humans have an EQ of 5.

As important as the increase in the relative size of the brain is the increase in its complexity. As the brain evolved its structures became more and more intricate. The cortex, the outer layer of nerve cells believed to be the seat of thinking and higher mental functions, became much thicker, and unfathomably complex. The brains of humans (and of whales and dolphins) are, with no exaggeration, the most complex structures in the known Universe – many times more complex than the largest computers such brains have yet designed.

This explosive development of the brain, occurring in just a few hundred thousand years, is one of the most dramatic and rapid changes in the whole of biological evolution. And on it rests the whole future of evolution. For through the human brain have come new creative potentials and new arenas for growth and development.

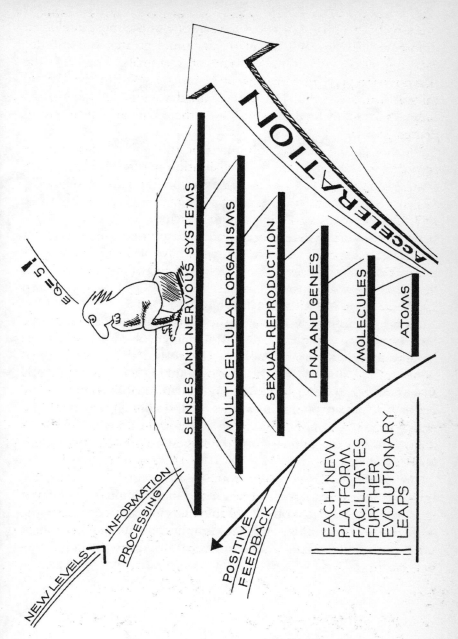

LANGUAGE
– THE DAWN OF THOUGHT

Man is nothing but evolution become conscious of itself.

Julian Huxley

To the casual observer the most noticeable difference between human beings and the great apes is not our larger brains, but the uses to which we put them. Unlike chimpanzees or gorillas – and unlike any other creature on Earth – human beings wear clothes, grow food, paint pictures, sing songs, dig wells, mine coal, read books, go to school, get married, remember anniversaries, earn money, maintain police forces, go to discotheques, hoard gold, hold elections, employ lawyers, belong to unions, go on holiday, follow fashion, join fan-clubs, collect stamps, give parties, fly planes, build highways, spray insecticides, build nuclear weapons, and worship God.

Such differences stem from human beings' ability to think, to reason, to be aware of ourselves, to make choices, and to purposefully modify the world around us. Each of these abilities depends in turn upon our exceptional capacity for language. Having brains several times larger than we need for our bodily functions gave us the added capacity necessary for the extremely complex neural processing involved in verbal communication.

Before this potential could be turned into speech, however, we needed a voice. Being able to make sounds is not by itself enough – most animals do that very well. Nor is the possession of a larynx, or 'voice-box,' sufficient; the great apes have well-developed larynxes. What makes the human larynx different are some important changes that it undergoes early in life.

At birth the human larynx, like that of the apes, is high in the throat, and in its first year a child's speech is restricted, and the sounds it makes are very reminiscent of those made by young chimpanzees. But during the second year the larynx descends to a lower position, carrying the base of the tongue with it. This change allows the tongue much greater freedom, and the child can begin to articulate a wide range of complex sounds. Speech becomes possible.

Learning as a Species

From an evolutionary perspective, speech represented a major step forward in information processing, as significant as the emergence of DNA, the evolution of sex, or the development of nervous systems. Each of these established a new platform for evolution, allowing learning to spread further and faster. Speech became an equally important platform. We could begin to share our discoveries with each other, learning not only from our experience, but also from the experiences of others – from those around us and from those who had gone before.

No longer did each individual have to build up knowledge of the world from scratch; we could begin to pool our experience. We had become a single learning system.

Rather as a multicellular organism continues beyond the life of its constituent cells – most of the cells that now compose your body will have died in a few years – language linked humanity into a multi-being system: an evolving community of minds whose collective learning lives on despite the death of its individual members.

And, just as the earlier development of sexual reproduction, by speeding the rate at which genetic changes could spread through a population, speeded the rate of biological evolution a thousandfold, so did language speed the rate at which we learnt. But with one significant difference. Genes carried information down lines of biological descendancy; language had no such constraints. Ideas could spread across a generation, leading to much greater cross-fertilization and another major quickening in the pace of evolution.

Accelerated Learning

Estimating the rate of growth in our collective knowledge is a difficult task. One inspired attempt has been that of the French economist Georges Anderla for the Organization for Economic Cooperation and Development.* He takes the known scientific facts of the year A.D.1 to represent one unit of collective human knowledge. Assuming that our collective learning began with language, it had taken approximately fifty thousand years for humanity to accrue that first unit.

According to Anderla's estimates, humanity had doubled its knowledge by A.D.1500. By 1750 total knowledge had doubled again; and by 1900 it had become 8 units. The next doubling took only fifty years, and the one after that only ten years, so that by 1960 humanity had gathered 32 units of knowledge. It then doubled again in the next seven years, and again in the following six years, taking us to 128 units in 1973, the year of Anderla's study.

There is no indication that this acceleration has slowed since then. It has almost certainly continued to increase ever-more rapidly. The French astrophysicist Dr. Jacques Vallée, for instance, has estimated that human knowledge is currently doubling *once every eighteen months*.

Whether or not one agrees with the details of Anderla's figures, the trend they reflect is very clear. As soon as our species gained the ability to pool its individual learnings our development moved ahead at an unprecedented rate. Never in the entire history of evolution on Earth had change been so fast.

A Thirst for Knowledge

Verbalization gave us the ability to think in words, to form concepts, and to have ideas. We could not only share our experiences, we could begin to think about them and understand them.

As we reflected upon our observations we discovered order in the world around. Not only did we see the stars, we saw that there were patterns in their movement. We could begin to draw conclusions and make predictions. Science had been born.

Endowed with one of the largest and most complex information

* Quoted in *Prometheus Rising* and elsewhere by Robert Anton Wilson.

processors on the planet, we searched for more and more learning. We were a species with a thirst for knowledge, a hunger to understand.

Through language we were able to ask questions. Why does night fall? How do the stars move? Where does rain come from? What makes the wind blow? Why do rivers flow? Why do plants grow?

Each question answered took us to a more intimate understanding of the Universe; and each answer left us with further questions. From where have we come? Why do we exist? Is there a meaning to life? Does creation have a purpose? From questions such as these came philosophy. And from their answers, religion.

Awakening to Time

Our capacity to think about our experience brought with it other changes. We became aware of time in a new way. We could think about past experiences, bringing them into the present moment. And we could think about future possibilities, bringing them too into the present. Our awareness expanded from the eternal 'now' into past and future. Time became a conscious thread in our lives, a dimension to our experience.

This dimension had a beginning and an end. We became aware of our own finiteness in time. And this greater awareness brought with it a price: we were able to envisage our own death. We began to fear the end of our experience – and of anything that reminded us of it. And we sought to know whether or not we continued after our bodies met their end. Was there an afterlife?

Awareness of time also expanded our choices. We could speculate about events that had not yet happened, judge whether or not they would be beneficial, consider alternatives and their consequences, and consciously choose our actions – and hence our futures.

Self-Reflective Consciousness

Being able to step back and reflect upon our experience gave humanity another distinctive ability. We became conscious of our own consciousness.

Consciousness itself was not new. Any creature that experiences the world around is conscious; but human beings are, as far as we know – we have not yet broken the communication barrier with dolphins and whales – the only creatures who recognize that they are conscious. We know that we know. We can observe our thoughts, experience our minds, and reflect upon our inner processes. We have a sense of self.

Having a sense of self, we can ask, 'Who am I?' 'What is consciousness?' We can begin to know how we know.

An Eye of the Universe

Evolution has come a long way – from the primordial energy of the Big Bang and subatomic particles, through atoms and molecules, to cells and organisms. On planet Earth it has now arrived at creatures with nervous systems so complex they can begin to understand the world in which they find themselves. Whether we are looking out at the stars, studying a flower or peering into a microscope, we are Life's way of exploring Creation; Nature's way of discovering and wondering at herself. Through us, through our senses and our minds, the Universe is beginning to discover itself, to become aware of its own existence.

We are an eye of the Universe.

We can look back over the whole evolutionary process and wonder at its magnificence. We can begin to understand the principles that led to our creation, and guess at where they might be leading. And, as we ponder the patterns of this long journey through time, Life – through us – becomes aware of its own becoming and possible purpose.

Furthermore, we are becoming conscious not only of the world around, but also of the world within, and of the consciousness that lights that world. As we awake to our own being, Life becomes aware of its own inner nature.

We are an 'I' of the Universe.

HANDS –
LEVERS FOR THE MIND

All tools and engines on earth are only extensions of
man's limbs and senses.

Ralph Waldo Emerson

Homo sapiens' capacity for symbolic language and conceptual thinking may have enabled us to learn from each other's experience, to
study the Universe, to plan our futures and to become aware of our
own existence, but these developments alone do not account for the
many changes in our lifestyle that so distinguish us from all other
animals. There is another unique feature of the human being that is
essential to our prolific creativity – the opposable thumb.

Chimpanzees, gorillas and several other creatures have thumbs,
but only the human thumb can rotate fully about its base, allowing
it to be put in direct opposition to each of the fingers. This unique
feature allows us to grasp objects of varying shapes and sizes,
manipulate them, and perform delicate operations with them. It
transforms the human hand into one of the most elegant and
versatile biological organs ever evolved.

Combine this beautiful evolutionary development with an ability
to reason and make choices, and you have a creature that can mold
the clay of Mother Earth into a variety of tools.

Tools themselves were not new to Nature – apes, for example,
will use stones as hammers, and so will some birds. Human beings,
however, endowed both with remarkable hands and with flourish-
ing minds, became the most proficient and prolific tool-users on the
planet. We moved from pots and hammers to boats, plows, wheels,
mills, drills, engines, planes, computers, robots, and space vehicles.

Through our hands ideas could manifest and take shape. We could
invent new forms. We could change the world in ways no other

creature could. We gained the power to influence our own future.

Such abilities constituted the second important platform on which human evolution was built. They led to a most remarkable series of inventions, unprecedented in the history of life on Earth – and all in the blink of an evolutionary eye.

Amplification of the Thumb

One of our earliest inventions was agriculture. We began to irrigate the land, plant seeds and store the harvest. Guaranteed a more reliable source of food, we were that much freer from the caprices of Nature. We could ensure against floods or droughts, settle in one place, and build permanent shelters.

We discovered that through selective breeding we could create new varieties of plants and animals. This enabled us to accelerate evolution, and to direct its course. In just a few thousand years we had produced hundreds of different cereals from just a few simple grasses, and a thousand different breeds of wolf – not to mention the many varieties of fruits, vegetables, horses, cattle and sheep.

About the same time we made another important discovery – how to control fire. All life's energy comes from the sun. Plants capture this energy through photosynthesis, and pass it on down the food chain to animals. This provides the energy we require to walk, to talk, and to plant the crops that caught the sunlight. By burning wood and other plant material, we had at our disposal another means of liberating the energy stored up by plants over many years. We could continue to warm ourselves even when the sun was down; we could survive cooler winters and expand our territory. Being able to cook food expanded our diets. And metals could be smelted to make more sturdy tools.

Several thousand years later came the wheel, creating both a revolution in transport and a wealth of new technology. The potter's wheel, the waterwheel, the windmill, the spinning wheel, the pulley, and most of the machinery humanity has ever invented were founded upon it.

The Industrial Revolution integrated the efficiency of the wheel with the energy of fire. Steam power replaced animal power and led to factories and mass production. Rail transport speeded communication, and made resources and products more easily available. Steel led to revolutions in engineering. Pumps facilitated the mining of coal and minerals we could not otherwise have reached. The mechanization of farming relieved many of the need to work on the land.

Here again positive feedback was at work. New discoveries led to new machinery and equipment – and these to other new discoveries. Efficient pumps paved the way for hydraulic power, giving us the ability to apply great pressure and move heavy loads. Precision engineering increased the reliability of scientific apparatus. As we understood more about the structure of matter we were able to create new materials – alloys, ceramics, plastics and other synthetics – with new properties. These could be used to create yet better machine components, more efficient manufacturing processes and a wealth of new products.

Electricity brought energy directly to the doors of factories and households across the country, providing an easy source of light and heat, and the power for a whole new generation of motors – large motors that enhanced the performance of industry, and smaller motors that led to a wide range of labor-saving machinery such as drills, washing machines, vacuum cleaners, electric mixers and toothbrushes.

In the arena of transport, steamships gathered resources from the four corners of the planet; the internal combustion engine made personal transport an affordable commodity; and the aeroplane compressed travel times from weeks to hours.

Everything was accelerating: movement, communication, energy consumption, production, social development. We were creating more and more change with less and less human effort.

Moreover, the rate of innovation was itself accelerating. In the early days of civilization major breakthroughs were few and far between. Buckminster Fuller estimates that about five thousand years ago a significant invention occurred every two hundred years or so. By A.D. 0 there was one every fifty years. By A.D. 1000 the time had shortened to thirty years, and in the Renaissance dropped sharply to around three years. With the advent of the Industrial Revolution it was down to a significant invention every six months; and a hundred years later, only three months. By the middle of the twentieth century the time had shortened further, and humanity was creating major breakthroughs at the rate of one per month. Mind's leverage on the world had multiplied a millionfold.

Some of our innovations are truly awe-inspiring; others justify concern and anxiety. Yet, magnificent or fearful as it may be, all of our technology is, in essence, the amplification of the potential inherent in the human hand – guided by the human mind.

INFORMATION –
THE CURRENCY OF CULTURE

To get to know each other on a world-wide scale is the
human race's most urgent need today.

Arnold Toynbee

Our hands and the technologies they spawned amplified our ability
to communicate and share our experiences. The result has been a
revolution in the circulation of information that may, from an
evolutionary perspective, turn out to be the most significant of all
our breakthroughs.

The trend towards higher orders of information processing is, as
we have seen, a pattern to be found throughout evolution. DNA,
sexual reproduction, senses and nervous systems had each, in their
own way, expanded Life's ability to collect, process, and store
information. Human language took this trend a stage further,
giving us the ability to learn from each other.

Limited to speech alone ideas could not travel far without
distortion or loss. So, some six thousand or more years ago, we
turned our hands to writing, starting with simple pictographs. This
enabled us to make more permanent records of our experiences and
share them with others down through time.

Initially we recorded our ideas on slabs of stone, which were
difficult to transport. The development of the pen and of papyrus
overcame this handicap. Our learnings could then be shared with
others in distant lands.

Two-and-a-half thousand years later, alphabetic writing was
born. New words could be created, and more abstract thoughts
expressed.

Convenient as they were, manuscripts had to be copied by hand –

a process that was both slow and prone to error. This drawback was overcome with the invention of the printing press, 550 years ago. Over the next half-century eight million books were produced. The philosophies of the Greeks and Romans were distributed, the Bible became widely accessible, and through various 'how to' books the skills of many crafts were disseminated, paving the way to the Renaissance.

The development of the telegraph in the early 1800s made it possible for the written word to be sent across vast distances. This was followed fifty years later by the telephone, linking people through the spoken word. The time to convey a message across the world had dropped from months to seconds.

Twenty-five years later the 'wireless' freed people from the need to be linked by cable in order to communicate. Information could be cast broadly and made available to multitudes simultaneously.

Then came the phonograph, television, tape recording and photocopying; each amplifying further our ability to circulate information.

With so much data at our fingertips, extra processing power was needed. So we turned to 'electronic brains.' More data than any human brain could ever entertain could be scanned, analyzed, evaluated, selected, and presented for inspection . . . and in seconds.

This enhanced processing capacity had a positive feedback on material technology. It enabled us to design and build larger and more complex items – bridges, aircraft, dams, buildings, tunnels, boats, engines. High technology could be guided and controlled – leading the way to the workerless factory, and opening the door into space.

And the progressive unfolding of technology further advanced our ability to gather and process information. Progress fed back on itself in an ever-tightening spiral. Never before in the history of Earth has the rate of innovation been so great.

Ephemeralization

Not only are we doing more, we are doing it with less and less – a process that the inventor Buckminster Fuller called 'ephemeralization.' The dome of St Peter's Basilica in Rome – the largest of its time – took 5,000 tons of stone and forty years to build. Today we

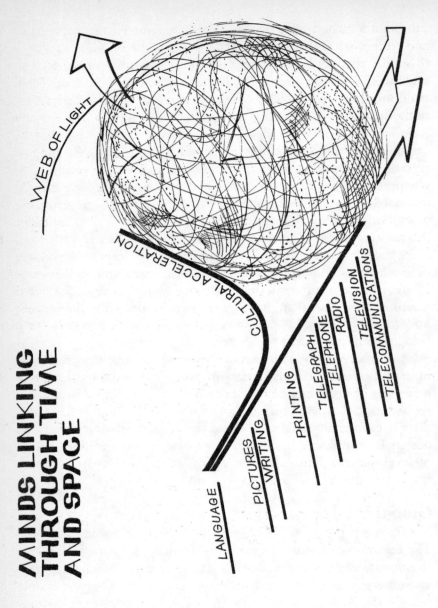

MINDS LINKING
THROUGH TIME
AND SPACE

WEB OF LIGHT

CULTURAL ACCELERATION

LANGUAGE
PICTURES
WRITING
PRINTING
TELEGRAPH
TELEPHONE
RADIO
TELEVISION
TELECOMMUNICATIONS

can build a carbon-fibre geodesic dome weighing only a few tons, and erect it in less than a week.

Similar changes have occurred in communication. A quarter-ton satellite can relay more information between Europe and North America than 175,000 tons of copper cable – and using a fraction of the energy.

As successive generations of computers moved from the switching of relays to the switching of vacuum tubes to the switching of crystals (and soon, possibly, to the switching of molecules), so computers have very rapidly decreased in size, and equally rapidly increased in power. A portable 'laptop' of 1990 has more memory, more flexibility, more functions, more versatility, and is far faster than any computer in existence in 1960.

As the power-to-size ratio of computers has exploded so have their numbers. When the first computers were built in the mid-1940s, it was estimated that the total world market for such machines was less than ten. Twenty-five years later there were 15,000 in existence. Fifteen years later 50,000 computers were being manufactured *each day*.

Since information itself is much more ephemeral than matter – indeed, it is virtually immaterial – it takes far less effort to create a new piece of software than it does to build a new piece of hardware. As a result, computer programs are now developing much faster than computers themselves. There are even computer programs designed to help in the writing of new programs. Keeping abreast of developments in this area now means updating every month.

Global Interconnection

The communications revolution also furthered humanity's integration into a single learning system. The potential to exchange ideas and experiences that began with the emergence of language is now worldwide. Artificial satellites, fiber optics, digital coding, computerized switching, faxes, video links and other advances in telecommunications have woven an ever-thickening web of information flowing around the world – billions of messages shuttling back and forth at the speed of light. We, the billions of minds of this huge 'global brain' are being linked together by the 'fibers' of our telecommunications systems in much the same way as are the billions of cells in our own brain.

Through this rapidly growing network of light we can share ideas and experiences not just with those around us, but with anyone, anywhere on the planet.

We are moving beyond civilization in its literal sense of 'making into towns' – into globalization. We are moving into a world without walls where distance is no separation. Today I can call up a friend on another continent and have as close a conversation as I could with someone in the same room – so close in fact that I can easily forget that our bodies are separated by thousands of miles.

Or I can send them a fax as easily as I can slip a note under a neighbor's door.

No longer is physical proximity necessary for a sense of community. The new technologies have transcended those earlier limitations. We can now communicate across the planet – mind to mind.

This emerging global brain also has global senses. A video camera in Beijing can instantly relay events to anyone who has the means to watch. A microphone in the Brazilian rainforest can allow people across the world to listen to the life abounding there. And sensors aboard a space probe can relay back to Earth views of the Solar System that no human eye has ever seen – one of our first and best-remembered collective experiences.

The eyes and ears of our telecommunications network are becoming the eyes and ears of humanity, allowing us to share new sets of experiences. And as our experiences expand so does our awareness of ourselves and our environment. We are becoming increasingly aware that we are all fellow passengers on 'Spaceship Earth.' We are a single species, sharing not only a common home, but also a common destiny.

A Global Consciousness

And maybe – just maybe – this global brain has its own global consciousness. Neuropsychologists suspect that the experiences and feelings that arise in our own minds are somehow related to the incredibly complex patterns of information flowing among the billions of cells in our brains. Who is to say that the same may not be happening at the global level?

Perhaps the similarly complex patterns of information flowing among the billions of nodes of our worldwide communication network is giving rise to some sort of awareness at the planetary level. If so, who knows what will happen as this web of light grows yet more complex and more brilliant? Maybe there could be some sort of awakening on the planetary level akin to our self-consciousness – or even surpassing it.

And who is to say how that might affect us. Might we feel some effects within our own minds? Might we find some greater guidance coming from this new consciousness – a consciousness that in some senses represents our collective mind? Only time will tell.

CREATIVITY –
FROM GENES TO IDEAS

If I had to define life in a word, it would be Life is
creation.

Claude Bernard

Humanity's unprecedented powers of both thought and action
have established us as a most significant species on planet Earth.
But our evolutionary significance does not end there. Our minds
and hands represent a new source of 'newness,' putting at Nature's
disposal a fundamentally new mechanism of evolution.

We may still be evolving biologically, but such developments are
occurring over much longer time-scales than our cultural growth.
From the perspective of human civilization they are imperceptible.
Indeed, the fact that our societies have removed many of the natural
pressures for biological evolution would suggest that any biological
changes that may be taking place are probably doing so even more
slowly than before.

What now determines our development is not our genes but our
ideas. Our mental faculties of understanding, reason and choice,
combined with the physical ability to turn ideas into form, have
opened to us a new means of adaptation. If people move to a cold
climate they no longer have to adapt by evolving a thicker coat of
hair, more fat, or changes in metabolism – a process that, even with
selective breeding, could take thousands of years. Instead they can
design and build insulated houses, central-heating systems, and
warmer clothing. If we choose to fly we can study aerodynamics
and build wings for ourselves; we do not need to go through the
long slow process of biological evolution that birds and flying insects
did. And if we want to step into the vacuum of space we can conceive
and create ways to take essential life-support systems with us.

A New Source of Novelty

It may not be easy to accept that our technological breakthroughs are also part of evolution. This is largely because twentieth-century scientific thinking considers evolution only in terms of the development of different biological species and the underlying genetic processes. Yet prior to Darwin the word 'evolution' had a much wider general usage. Its original meaning is the 'rolling out' of the world: the emergence of new forms and phenomena from existing ones. In those days the term was applied to the world in general – including the world of ideas – rather than just to living creatures.

Prior to biological evolution there had been, as we saw in the first chapter, an evolution of matter. New atomic elements were created from combinations of existing atoms; and as these formed into compounds, new substances emerged bringing new properties to matter. Only later, after the material Universe had evolved into very large and complex molecules capable of self-reproduction, did genetic processes begin molding the clay into a rich variety of living forms. Now, with the appearance of *Homo sapiens*, a new form of evolution has become possible. It is our minds and hands that are doing the molding, reorganizing matter into new structures and creating new capacities.

Mind has now become the dominant creative force on this planet. The whole panorama of change that humanity has initiated, the whole of the culture that differentiates us from every other creature on this planet, started as ideas in the mind.

We are, quite literally, 'making stuff up' – first in our minds, then in the physical world.

This shift from genes to ideas represents not just another step in biological evolution, but a giant leap for evolution itself – a fundamentally new platform for development. Through us the Universe is not only able to observe and explore itself, it can also reach out and consciously influence its own development. A brave new power of creativity is at Life's fingertips. And we, the products of its evolution, have now become conscious participants in the continuing unfolding of creation.

Unnatural Creations?

Many think that humanity's creations are not 'natural' in the way that the creations of biological evolution are. Why is this? We do not consider a beehive to be less natural than a bee, nor a beaver's dam less natural than a beaver. Why should creations that come through the human mind and hand be any less natural?

Why do we think a lamp post is less natural than a tree? It is true that they were created in two different ways; one is a product of biological processes, the other a design of the human mind. One is a living system and the other inanimate. We may judge one more beautiful than the other. But are they any different in the eyes of the Universe? Both are experiments in design. Both are the result of eons of evolution.

The different way we perceive many human artifacts stems from the effects they have on the world. When these effects do not seem to be in harmony with the rest of Nature we regard them as 'unnatural.'

Paradoxical as it may seem, the root of this disharmony lies in the very fact that we *do not* recognize ourselves and our creations as a natural part of evolution. Our unique powers incline us to see ourselves as different from the rest of Nature rather than an integral part of it. This has been reinforced by Western scientific 'objectivity' that, in seeking to understand the world of which we are a part, has set us apart from it.

This separation may be only in our minds, but it has profound effects. As we shall see later, the assumption that we are somehow different leads to a particular set of values. Believing we are masters of Nature, rather than agents within it, we use our unprecedented creative potential for our own perceived ends, resulting in actions that do indeed separate us from the rest of Nature.

In short, our creativity may frequently be misguided; but it is not unnatural.

Not in a Billion Years

Evolution mediated by human minds and hands has been able to create in years developments that would have taken genetic processes alone millions of years – or might never have occurred at all. The solar cell, for example, represents a totally new method of capturing the sun's energy – converting it directly into electricity. This is as significant a breakthrough as the development of photosynthesis itself, some three billion years ago.

Radar has allowed us to 'see' at new ranges of frequencies – a development as significant as the evolution of the eye.

Through nuclear physics we have discovered how to create new chemical elements. The last time that such a synthesis occurred in our area of the Universe was in the supernova that preceded our sun, some five billion years ago.

Genetic engineering allows us to create new species of life. The creation of new organisms is no longer solely dependent upon the slow process of genetic evolution; we can consciously design and create them within a matter of months. (Though whether we will use this awesome power wisely remains to be seen.)

And we have made our first journeys out into space and walked on the moon – a step which biological evolution alone might never have achieved, not in ten billion years.

TODAY –
PLATFORM FOR TOMORROW

'A slow sort of country!' said the Queen. 'Now, here, you see, it takes all the running you can do, to keep in the same place. If you want to get somewhere else, you must run at least twice as fast as that!'

Lewis Carroll

The story so far: After billions of years of evolution there has emerged on planet Earth a creature with a self-conscious mind; a creature able to reflect upon its experience; a creature that can think, reason, and draw conclusions about the Universe in which it finds itself. That creature is us.

We are beings that can learn from each other's experience. We can ask questions and ponder the meaning of our existence. We are aware of the passing of time and conscious of our own end.

We are a species with aspirations, able to consider our actions, imagine their outcome and choose our own future. We are a species that educates its young and cares for its sick.

We are a species that can reshape the Earth. We have harnessed the energy of fire and liberated the energy of matter. We have amplified the power of our opposable thumb to the extent that one thumb could destroy us all. And we have refined the delicacy of the finger to the point of editing the molecules of life.

Seeking greater well-being we have modified our surroundings in a multitude of ways. We have traveled further and faster than any other species, survived in extremes of climate, and ventured into the void. Together we have created more change on this planet than any other creature at any other time.

Faster and Faster

All of this has come about in what, from an evolutionary viewpoint, is virtually no time at all. We are the product of an ever-tightening spiral of development that has condensed time-scales from billions of years to mere decades.

And there would seem to be no letting up. The factors behind this speeding up are as present today as they ever were. Advances in science, technology, communications, education, health care, and culture are all bound together in a single multi-dimensional feed-back loop. We are learning faster, growing faster, moving faster, and changing faster. In one year we may experience as many innovations as the pharaohs did in a century.

Looking to the future, one thing seems certain: whatever form development may take, its pace will continue to increase. New discoveries and new technologies will lead to other new abilities – new ways of expressing ideas and new ways of changing the world. Creativity will continue to breed creativity.

Saving Time

As if these pressures for further change were not enough, there is another factor that is fueling the increasing pace of life: our attitude to time. Much of humanity has become obsessed with time. This is particularly so in those cultures that have experienced the greatest leaps in material development. Believing that time can be 'saved,' we seek to pack more and more into the time available.

We shop in supermarkets to save the time it would take to visit several stores – and we like quick check-out lines. We build freeways around and through cities so that we can reduce journey times by fifteen minutes – and so pack a few more things into our day. We spend fortunes digging tunnels that will save us another half-hour. We set up electronic offices so that mail arrives imme-diately, replies are returned more speedily, decisions made faster – and more time saved. We construct noisy and polluting supersonic aircraft (and plan even faster ones) so that a very small minority can save a little more time.

Any development that can do something more quickly has an advantage in the marketplace. Seduced by the idea of temporal efficiency, we focus much of our creative talent on getting more and more done in less and less time. With the extra time we have 'saved' we pack in some more tasks – and then require another time-saving tool to cope.

However giddy today's rate of development may seem, tomorrow's world will – barring calamity – be changing even faster. And the world beyond that yet faster still.

Wherever Next?

But – where are we going? Where will our burgeoning creativity take us next? What will the World Trade Center's next layer of paint hold in store?

In the short term, technology will extend in some fairly predictable directions. Computers will become faster, smaller and more 'friendly,' pervading almost every area of life. Increasing miniaturization will lead to robots small enough to travel through the blood. Medical science may extend human life by another decade or two. Fibre optics and digital processing will transform the telephone into a multi-purpose tool that can handle data and images as easily as it now handles voice. Virtual reality will become commonplace. New superconductors will bring trains traveling at half the speed of sound. Genetic reprogramming will offer new treatments for otherwise incurable hereditary diseases – as well as new drugs, new foods, new insecticides, and various other things that humanity believes it must have.

Yet, at the same time as we push ahead towards greater technological brilliance, the dangers of misapplying our awesome powers are also becoming increasingly apparent. Life on planet Earth is suffering badly from the impact of our waste. Its mineral and biological resources have been plundered. And its delicately balanced climate is being disturbed – perhaps irreversibly.

Moreover, as resources dwindle the tensions between people increase, and threaten to explode at the slightest provocation. If we do not quickly recognize ourselves and our creations as an intrinsic part of Nature, there may well be no future at all for us.

And even if we do, the future will still be full of surprises. Who in 1900 would have predicted the solar cell, genetic engineering, nuclear weapons, radar, microchips, the personal computer, satellite navigation, lasers, television, videocassettes, pocket hi-fi, or many of the other breakthroughs that we today accept so easily?

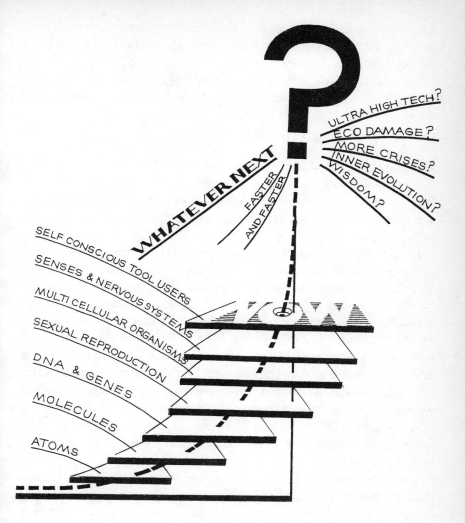

They were all beyond the thinking of the time. Most of them were still beyond our thinking half a century later.

Similarly, of the developments that lie ahead, we are likely to foresee only those that are extensions of our present thinking. Most of the breakthroughs yet to come still lie beyond our imagination. They remain, quite literally, inconceivable.

Inner Evolution

One area where we may see some of the most exciting developments is the exploration and development of human consciousness.

Consciousness is something that we all share. Yet its nature and its potential remain, by and large, a mystery. We still know very little about how sensory perception leads to awareness and how ideas come into being. We have very little understanding about our feelings, or the ways in which our attitudes affect our perception and behavior. And the self, that most intimate aspect of the conscious mind, remains as mysterious as ever.

This may be the next great frontier. Its exploration could lead to a wealth of 'inner technologies' – technologies concerned not with managing matter or information, but with the management of our own minds.

Some of these technologies may be physical. Biofeedback, for example, a process by which factors such as blood pressure or the electrical activity of the brain are turned into a visual or auditory signal that the subject tries to control by modifying his or her own state of mind, makes use of the sort of electronic technology that we have become used to. Whereas meditation – another effective technique of modifying one's state of consciousness – usually involves no material technologies at all.

Since serious exploration in this field has hardly begun, it would be unwise to make predictions as to the form of the inner technologies that we might develop. All that can be said is that they are likely to be techniques and processes that assist our mental functioning – help us think more clearly, remember better, clarify our perception, feel more fully, free ourselves from fear, release our creativity, communicate more clearly, and relate more honestly. They will be technologies that bring greater mastery of our minds, a greater awareness of our selves and a greater openness of heart.

As we shall see later, not only could this be the next step for humanity; it could be the next step for the evolution of life on Earth. It is possible that all of our development so far is simply paving the way for this inner exploration – the exploration not just of the mind, but of consciousness itself.

Our power to change the world may have made prodigious leaps, but our internal development – the development of our attitudes and values – has progressed much more slowly. We seem to be as prone to greed, aggression, short-sightedness, and self-centeredness as we were two-and-a-half thousand years ago when the Greeks were extolling their ethical philosophies and the virtues of self-knowledge. Many good words have been spoken over the years; but how many have been lived?

If we are to continue our evolutionary journey it is imperative that we now make some equally prodigious leaps in consciousness. We must develop the wisdom that will allow us to use our new powers for our own good – and for the good of all. This is the challenge of our times.

NOW
BUT NOT NOW

As you travel through these pages you may feel that you are entering a tunnel that ends in doom and disaster. Such a tunnel does indeed lie along the route we are traveling; but at the end of the tunnel is a light far more brilliant than that envisioned by even the most optimistic futurist. And it is towards this light that we are headed.

Toy-bewitched,
Made blind by lusts, disinherited of soul,
No common centre Man, no common sire
Knoweth! A sordid solitary thing
Mid countless brethren with a lonely heart
Through courts and cities the smooth savage roams,
Feeling himself, his own low self, the whole;
When he by sacred sympathy might make
The Whole one Self! Self that no alien knows,
Self, far diffused as fancy's wing can travel!
Self, spreading still! Oblivious of its own
Yet all of all possessing! This is Faith!
This is the Messiah's destined victory!

S.T. Coleridge, Religious Musings

JEOPARDY – THE FAILINGS OF SUCCESS

This we know – the earth does not belong to man, man belongs to the earth. All things are connected like the blood which unites one family. Whatever befalls the earth befalls the sons of the earth. Man did not weave the web of life; he is merely a strand in it. Whatever he does to the web, he does to himself.

Chief Seattle

We may be living through the most stimulating and exciting times in history; but our rapid development has brought with it unexpected dangers, not the least of which is humanity's ever-growing numbers.

Ten thousand years ago the human population numbered around ten million, gathered into small settlements. As we evolved the conditions of our lives improved and our numbers consequently grew. By A.D.1000 there were about 340 million of us. In 1650 the world population was around 545 million and by 1800 it was 900 million. Nineteenth-century advances in hygiene and medicine kept our numbers expanding, and by 1900 they had reached 1,600 million. By 1950 our population was 2,500 million, and in the next forty years it doubled to 5,000 million. There are now signs that this explosion is beginning to slow down. If current trends continue then our numbers will probably stabilize somewhere between 10,000 and 12,000 million – a dauntingly large figure, but one that is sustainable, provided that we are willing to tackle the various problems that follow in its wake.

Our rapidly expanding size has put many pressures on the world that sustains us. There are many more mouths to feed, bodies to clothe, and people to house. There are many more tools to manufacture, much more waste to dispose of, and much more energy required to do it all.

As if these were not problems enough, our technological development has magnified the demands made by each person. The average city-dweller of the late twentieth century consumes several hundred times the energy that a peasant farmer did a thousand years ago – and enjoys a higher standard of health, nourishment, and comfort than did even a king at that time.

As a result the total pressure we put upon the planet has increased even more rapidly than the population itself – a hundred times the people using a hundred times the resources amounts to ten thousand times the demand.

The Price of Fire

Nearly all the energy consumed by humanity has been obtained from the taming of fire – initially from the burning of wood, but later from dung, coal, oil, and gas. Before the dawn of civilization forests carpeted most of the land, and had wood been used only to keep us warm the land might have stayed that way. However, our developing technologies were also hungry for wood – wood to fire the kilns that produced pottery and bricks, wood to build houses and boats, wood to construct carts, plows, and other machinery. The result was deforestation.

The faster humanity developed, the more rapidly did the forests disappear. In Europe trees were felled to provide both fuel and timber, and the cleared areas became fields (the word is derived from 'felled') producing food for the growing population. As the European forests dwindled, the forests of North America were plundered – first New England, then the Midwest. An area the size of Europe was devastated in a few decades.

Today less than 20 percent of the Earth remains forested; yet our demand for wood is greater than it has ever been. The consequence, as we are all well aware, is the plundering of the largest remaining forests – the tropical rainforests. An area the size of England is being destroyed each year – and the rate is increasing.

No one really knows what the long-term effects will be. The rainforests are an important organ of the biosphere and exert a considerable influence on the Earth's weather. Moreover, the destroyed areas cannot easily be reclaimed. The soil that remains is relatively poor, and after a few years of grazing collapses into desert.

As we destroy the forests we also eradicate entire species of plants and animals. Current estimates suggest about ten thousand species become extinct every year – about one every hour. And the figure is growing. Yet the survival of life on Earth depends upon the rich diversity of its species. How many more can we destroy before the planet's biosystem collapses?

A Warmer World

The second price we had to pay for fire has been a warming we did not intend – global warming.

The principal waste product of fire is carbon dioxide. This is not in itself a dangerous gas; indeed it is crucial to the life of plants, and, given time, the biosphere could absorb all the carbon dioxide that we produce. The problem is that we are producing it far faster than the oceans and plants can absorb it. Half of the 20,000 million tons we now release each year remains in the air. Since the Industrial Revolution the carbon dioxide content of the atmosphere has risen by about a third – and most of that rise has occurred in the last few decades.

Although the concentration of carbon dioxide is small in absolute terms (about 0.03 percent), it has a significant effect on climate. Carbon dioxide allows heat from the sun in, but does not allow the Earth's heat, which is of a different wavelength, to radiate out so easily. This is what the glass in a greenhouse does – hence 'the greenhouse effect.' The more carbon dioxide there is, the more heat is trapped, and the warmer the atmosphere becomes. It is estimated that the northern hemisphere has warmed by nearly 1°C (2°F) this century, and could well warm by 2°C to 3°C (3½°F to 5½°F) over the next fifty years.

This may not sound much, but it is a lot for the Earth; and its full impact remains far from certain. As well as a probable rise in sea levels and the consequent flooding of lowland areas such as Bangladesh, the Netherlands, and many of the world's coastal cities, with all its ensuing problems and enormous costs, there are other possible consequences of even greater concern. Vegetation would not be able to 'migrate' as fast as the changes in climate; many temperate forests would vanish, adding further to climatic instability. Areas that we rely upon for much of our food, such as the grain prairies of the USA, may suddenly become arid. The consequences of widespread crop failure have already been tasted in areas such as the African Sahel, where for several seasons the rains have failed as a result of changes in global weather patterns. Shifts in climate may also lead to changes in ocean currents such as the Gulf Stream, which circulates heat from the tropics to Western Europe. If this were to occur countries such as Britain could be in for a dramatic cooling rather than a warming. At the moment, however, we simply do not know enough about the planet's climate to tell exactly what repercussions global warming will have.

There is even a school of thought that believes that a warming in the tropics may flip the climate near the poles into an Ice Age. As tropical air warms it takes up more water from the oceans. When it arrives at arctic regions, this more moist air could result in greater cloud cover. The ground beneath, more shielded from the sun, would cool, while the increased moisture would fall as more snow. Rather than melting, the ice caps could begin to spread. Paleoclimatologists estimate that recent Ice Ages have occurred on a regular cycle; roughly a hundred thousand years of ice, broken by warmer interglacial periods of about fifteen thousand years. The current warm period has given humanity the opportunity to populate latitudes closer to the poles, but this brief respite may now be coming to an end. The next Ice Age is due any time – any time within the next thousand years, that is – and a cooling of the poles could be just the trigger it needs. In that case we might find Scandinavia under ice while Italy dried out.

A new Ice Age is only one possible scenario. Many believe that global warming could put an end to Ice Ages altogether, and with far more catastrophic consequences. Even a modest global warming could trigger a runaway effect. Frozen in the tundras of northern Canada and Russia are vast amounts of a more potent greenhouse gas than carbon dioxide, methane. If these areas thaw, releasing their methane into the atmosphere, the world would warm much faster. And this is without the current doubling in methane produced by all the cows we keep, by the rice paddies that are growing in step with our population, by decomposing swamps, and by the termites that feed on the dead wood in our dying forests. Water vapor itself is a greenhouse gas; and as the air becomes warmer and more moist, the heat trapped in the tropical regions will increase yet further. Deforestation does not help either, reducing the biosphere's capacity to absorb carbon dioxide. Moreover, the warmer the world becomes the faster will dead vegetation decay, both on land and in the sea, further speeding the release of greenhouse gases.

As a result of these and other positive-feedback loops, the Earth's temperature may rise much more rapidly than initially suspected. Summarizing this runaway scenario in the British science magazine *New Scientist*, John Gribbin warned that if this happens 'the greenhouse threat facing us is worse than any forecaster has yet dared to imagine.'

Recipes for Disaster

Carbon dioxide is just one unwanted waste product of our industrialization. Automobiles, power stations and chemical plants pour poisonous gases into the atmosphere, to fall later as acid rain. As the acidity of rivers, lakes and soil rises, the fauna and flora suffer. In western Germany over half the trees have been affected, many of them killed, and the damage in Eastern Europe has been even more disastrous. In Scandinavia entire lakes are dead. And we are only just beginning to recognize the effects of acid rain on human beings.

Meanwhile we dump our chemical garbage out of sight under the soil, only to find it later seeping into our water supplies. Or we pour it into the sea, killing not just fish but other organisms crucial to the ecological balance.

As if this were not enough, short-sighted intensive agricultural practices turn soil into sterile dust to be washed or blown away. At present rates of loss of twenty six billion tons per year – that is five tons *per person* per year – there will be nothing left in a hundred years.

Most dangerous of all, the ozone layer in the upper atmosphere, which protects life on land from the Sun's damaging ultraviolet rays, is being destroyed by the chlorofluorocarbon (CFC) gases released from aerosols, refrigerators, air conditioners, and some fast-food packaging. With CFCs we have done more than release a pollutant; we have released a catalyst – a substance that speeds up other reactions without itself being changed. One molecule of a CFC can destroy tens of thousands of ozone molecules, and continue doing so for many decades before it is itself destroyed.

Even if CFC production were eliminated immediately and completely – which given current attitudes is not very likely – the gases released during the past two decades will continue to wreak their havoc for another fifty years or more.

The damaging effects of increased ultraviolet light could be catastrophic – skin cancers would be the least of our worries. Blind insects, for instance, would not be very good at pollinating plants. This would have instant ramifications for the planet's food chain – and ours. In addition, particular frequencies of ultraviolet light damage DNA molecules, leading to cellular malfunctions and mutations.

Worse still, life on land could become impossible. For half a million years the ozone layer has shielded the Earth from ultraviolet light, making it possible for plants and animals to emerge from the sea and colonize the land. Without this protection life would forced back beneath the surface of the sea – such life that survived, that is.

Other Threats

It need not be environmental disasters that claim us. As the peoples of the world become ever-more intimately linked we become increasingly vulnerable to plagues. Some years ago scientists working for the U.S. Government conducted a simple experiment. They sprayed harmless bacteria into the departure lounge of Washington's National Airport. Hitching rides on the passengers and transferring at their destination on to others, the bacteria spread from person to person. Within three weeks they were to be found in nearly every corner of the U.S.A.

We should count ourselves lucky that AIDS is not spread as easily – we would all have been infected before the first case had been diagnosed. (Although given the extremely high mutation rate of the AIDS virus, we should not count our chickens too soon.) And who knows what other diseases are lurking, waiting for the right conditions in order to become epidemic; or what diseases we might inadvertently create through genetic engineering? Moreover, should a new plague appear, our over-enthusiasm for antibiotics has left our bodies weakened and our medical armory that much poorer. With the passing of time our vulnerability rises rather than falls.

Finally we should not overlook the ecological effects of war.

Military operations consume much of the world's oil production, and many of the Earth's resources. Nor is modern warfare very good for the planet. Agent orange, napalm, biological weapons, and high explosives have a far more devastating impact than bows and arrows and cannonballs. Although there has not been a World War for fifty years, the number of small wars is steadily increasing – currently about fifteen per year.

And although we have so far managed to avoid a nuclear war, it remains an ever-present danger. As resources become less plentiful, food more scarce, the gap between rich and poor grows, and climatic change promotes mass migrations, it is not difficult to imagine a number of scenarios leading, either accidentally or deliberately, to a nuclear holocaust. If such a disaster were to occur it would almost certainly bring an end to our accelerating development.

The Totally Unexpected

As likely as any of these scenarios are those that remain totally unexpected. The appearance of the ozone hole over Antarctica was a surprise. Scientists had known for twenty years that CFCs would deplete the ozone layer, but none of their models had predicted an ozone hole, nor did the idea feature among any of their hunches. Indeed, so surprising was the data that the computers analyzing it systematically rejected it for several years.

Our knowledge of ecology and global climate still contains so many gaps and grey areas that other wholly unanticipated changes are virtually certain. There may be unforeseen flips in the weather; unexpected changes in ecosystems; surprising responses by other species; unpredicted earthquakes in significant locations; or new discoveries that change our whole thinking. Whatever they may be, let us hope that when the unexpected comes we will have the inner flexibility and stability to cope with it wisely.

CROSSROADS – CHOOSING OUR WAY

No problem can be solved from the same consciousness that created it.

Albert Einstein

To an extent the environmental crisis has been inevitable. As soon as we combined the energy of fire with the power of technology we embarked upon a fateful course. But we embarked upon it with the best of intentions. We were applying our creativity to the task of improving the quality of our lives. We were seeking a longer and more comfortable existence. And there can be no blame for that.

It is only now as we realize the many ways in which our best intentions have backfired that we need to correct our behavior. We have the opportunity to respond to the crisis we have inadvertently created. Yet the will to respond seems curiously lacking. Instead we rush headlong towards catastrophe.

The closing pages of Emile Zola's novel, *The Beast in Man*, come to mind. A train full of soldiers on the way to war is rushing downhill, while the driver and fireman are having a fight. The fireman insists on stoking the engine, and the driver is trying to stop him. As they tussle, one grabs the other by the throat and together they tumble off the engine – leaving the train-load of drinking and singing soldiers hurtling downhill, totally unaware of what has happened. And there the book ends!

We seem to be in a rather similar situation. We are hurtling at an ever-accelerating pace towards disaster, and with no one in the driving seat. The one significant difference is that we are not unaware of the dangers ahead. It is as if the conductor has come back down the train announcing that we are out of control, and we still sit playing cards. We hear the bad news, but for one reason or another – perhaps because we are too numbed by the news, feel so powerless, or are too concerned with our selves – we continue as if it will all turn out fine.

What we seem to lack is the will to get out of our seats and try together to avoid disaster. We lack the courage to face the truth. Most of us appear more concerned with defending ourselves against our fellow passengers. Or with making sure that we win our game.

The Will to Change?

We do not lack the science and technology to tackle most of the problems facing us. In almost every area we know what needs to be done to restore the environment and keep it in a healthy state; and where we do not yet have the necessary means, we know how to set about developing it.

Nor are we short of the money needed to mend the world. The WorldWatch Institute in Washington D.C. has estimated that the total cost of a six-year program to protect the soil, reforest the land, reduce population growth, retire the debts of the developing countries, raise energy efficiency, and develop renewable sources of energy would amount to around $750,000 million. A lot, yes; but no more than the world currently spends on arms in just *one* year! All that we lack is the will.

Are we prepared to reconsider our priorities?

Can we stop destroying the rainforests, now, before it is too late? And who is responsible? Is it the hamburger-eaters and the timber-hungry industries who encourage farmers to cut down the forest and use it as pasture for a few years? The governments that allow this to happen? The banks that demand an interest on their loan? Or all of us?

Can we stop pouring carbon dioxide into the skies; or do we love our energy-hungry lifestyle too much? Can we significantly reduce our use of fossil fuels; or are we too attached to our current technologies and to the comforts they bring?

Can we stop acid rain? Or is the momentum of industrialization too great?

Will we stop destroying the ozone layer? Or will a total ban on the offending chemicals prove too 'impractical?'

What will it take for us to change the way we farm the land, to put as much in as we take out? Do the short-term economic and practical considerations of such change make it near impossible?

What of the 90 percent of humanity who have not yet enjoyed the benefits of 'development.' Can we expect them not to want to join the party – especially when at last it seems within their reach?

Which brings us to the essential question behind all these questions. Why does humanity as a whole continue to behave in ways that are clearly not in its best interest? Where is the will to change?

What's wrong with us?

MADNESS –
A BUG IN THE MIND?

The crew of spacecraft Earth is in virtual mutiny to the
order of the universe.

Edgar Mitchell

How, we must ask, does a species that has developed reason,
foresight and choice come to behave in such short-sighted ways?
How come we can be both so intelligent and so stupid? Are we
really as clever as we like to believe?

How intelligent is a species that can take several thousand square
miles of fertile land, name it after 'the queen of the angels,' then
cover it with concrete, pollute the air, banish most other living
creatures, and pay vast sums of money to live in it?

How intelligent is a species that can be aware that there is more
to life than meets the eye, that can talk of the oneness of all
humanity and the supremacy of love, and then turn this wisdom
into doctrines that it defends by killing those who describe this
oneness and love in slightly different terms?

How intelligent is a species that can understand it is destroying
the ecosystem crucial for its existence – and then continues to
destroy it? Any individual who behaved in such an irrational
manner, without any care or respect for its own welfare or that of
others, would be classed as insane.

A Planetary Cancer

Humanity's less-than-intelligent behavior towards its surroundings
is somewhat reminiscent of cancer. Cancers can reproduce very fast

and with no regard for the rest of the organism. They are a part of the body, yet in many respects behave as if they were completely separate. They are also stupid, destroying the very system upon which they are totally dependent.

Similarly, the human population has been growing rapidly, and with little regard for its environment. We are a part of the Earth's biosphere, and totally dependent upon it, yet we continue to behave as if we were apart from it. Our cities eat into the countryside, eradicating natural ecosystems, spreading deserts of sand and concrete. We allow our toxic wastes to flow into our surroundings, poisoning other species with hardly a blink. And we too are short-sighted. For if we continue along this path we are likely to cause irreversible damage to the biosphere, and will probably destroy ourselves.

But the parallels go deeper than surface appearances and behavior. When we look at what underlies cancer and at what underlies humanity's malignant tendencies, we again find remarkably similar patterns.

In essence cancer can be thought of as a programming error. The genes in the heart of every cell are essentially a set of chemical programs that give instructions on how to construct various complex proteins; the number and type of proteins that are built determines the cell's structure and behavior. Although virtually every cell in your body contains the same set of instructions, only those appropriate to that type of cell and its current phase of development are turned on at a given time.

Sometimes, however, sets of instructions that should be 'off' get turned 'on,' or vice versa. This can happen for a number of reasons. Radiation from space, nuclear reactors, or medical treatments may damage the control sequences – the switches in the gene. Toxic chemicals in the air, in water, or in food, may produce changes in the molecular information. Or a virus may enter the cell and insert itself into a gene, disrupting its sequence of instructions. Guided by an inappropriate set of programs, the damaged cell no longer acts in harmony with the rest of the body. It becomes a 'rogue' cell.

Generally the results are benign. But if instructions to grow and multiply are turned on the rogue cell can begin proliferating. This is the beginning of cancer.

An Error in Our Software

Humanity's malignant tendencies can also be considered as programming errors. However, the shift from biological evolution to cultural evolution means that the 'programs' that now influence our behavior and development are to be found not in our genes but in our minds. They are our attitudes and values – the way we see life, the way we see ourselves and what we think is important. It is these, not our genes, that determine our decisions and day-to-day activity. And it is here that our errors lie.

We may, for instance, take the attitude that our own benefit comes before that of others. We may imagine that we can own the land, own the Earth's resources, and even own other creatures. We may value our material possessions more for the status they bring than for their utility. And we may believe that financial or political expediency is more important than our long-term welfare.

Taking the parallel with cancer a little further, one might say that a 'virus' has entered the human mind. A set of errant mental programs has mutated human consciousness, inclining us towards self-centeredness and short-sightedness, and disturbing our collective sanity.

How has this happened? What is the origin of this dysfunctional thinking?

Arthur Koestler has argued that somewhere along our evolutionary journey human beings developed a 'hardware fault.' Our brains became 'mis-wired', leading us to be born with an inherently selfish nature. If so, there would seem to be little hope – apart perhaps from neurosurgery or some new drug.

There is, however, another possibility. The underlying fault may be a 'software problem' – a 'bug' in our thinking. We shall see shortly that, like the genes in a malignant cell that are switched on inappropriately, some of our mental programs appear to be active when they would better be turned off.

NEEDS –
SURVIVAL OF THE SELF

Happiness belongs to those who are sufficient unto
themselves. For all external sources of happiness are, by
their very nature, highly uncertain, precarious,
ephemeral, and subject to chance.

Arthur Schopenhauer

Of all our innate drives, the most fundamental is that for physical
survival. It is a basic instinct to avoid danger and seek safety.
Without it humankind would almost certainly have become extinct
long ago.

This drive ensures that we satisfy our physiological needs for air,
water, and food – needs that are essential for the continuation of
our biological selves. When these are satisfied we are free to take
care of other bodily requirements, such as those for rest, warmth,
shelter, and protection. Although of lesser priority, they are still
very important for our continued existence and well-being.

Once our individual day-to-day survival has been attended to, we
can fulfill other less urgent, but equally important needs – such as
that for reproduction, which ensures the survival of the species.

As Abraham Maslow demonstrated some forty years ago, our
various needs are arranged as a hierarchy. Needs lower down the
hierarchy take priority, but once satisfied we are free to move on to
progressively higher levels of need.

Psychological Needs

Once our various physical requirements have been taken care of we
do not, like many animals, simply curl up and rest. As self-conscious

entities we have further needs. Capable of thinking ahead, we wish to know that our future is secure. Able to make choices about our future, we want to feel in control of things. As part of a community the way that others perceive us matters – we want to be recognized and approved of. Aware of our own potential, we like to feel a measure of self-esteem. And, conscious of our own self, we have a need for identity – to know who we are.

As with our physical needs, these psychological needs are important for our survival. They have played a critical role in our development as a species. Recognition and approval, for instance, have helped us fit in to our social group; while the need for security has helped us avoid dangerous situations and maintain access to natural resources that enable us to meet future bodily needs.

These inner needs have also been valuable in our development as individuals. As we grew up they helped us relate to the world, adapt to the culture in which we found ourselves, and develop a sense of self.

Although we may occasionally have to attend to lower levels of the hierarchy, most of us in the more developed world are driven by our psychological needs more than our physical ones. It is these psychological needs that lie behind most of our desires. The need for security, for example, often manifests as the desire for wealth – although money can also confer a sense of status. Much of our social behavior is geared towards gaining the approval and recognition of others – as are many of our possessions. The foods we eat are often chosen more for their stimulation of the taste buds than their nutritional value – and if they can be consumed in classy restaurants, so much the better. And the desire for sex, more often than not, is a reflection not of a biological need but of one or more of our inner needs – self-esteem, attention, approval, intimacy, love, security, control, power, excitement.

No Satisfaction

Most of us try to satisfy these psychological needs through our interaction with the world. We seek inner fulfillment through what we have or what we do, through the experiences the world provides, and through the way others behave towards us. But this seldom seems to provide any lasting satisfaction.

A person may gather a great deal of wealth, but is he really more secure? More than likely he will soon find new sources of insecurity. Are my investments safe? Will the stock-market crash? Can I trust my friends? Should I employ *security* companies to protect my possessions?

Someone else, seeking fulfillment through sensory stimulation, may at last discover the gastronomic excellence he has been searching for. Does that satisfy him? Or come the next day is he wondering when he might be able to repeat the experience?

Another may seek fame in order to be approved and accepted. Is she then happy? Or is she upset at having lost the love of her family, or no longer deriving any satisfaction from her work?

Others may chase after power. But this too can have the opposite effect, leading people – and sometimes nations – into conflicts over which they have very little control.

We may believe that if only we could find the right relationship we would be fulfilled. Thus we continually look around for the perfect person, the person who satisfies our expectations; the person who will satisfy our inner needs and so make us happy. Yet such fulfillment can be short-lived. It may not be long before we start finding imperfections in even the most perfect person.

Part of the problem is that we are looking for fulfillment in a world that is constantly changing – and changing ever more rapidly. Stock-markets go up and down, cars get bumped, fashions come and go, friends change their minds. Any satisfaction we do gain is likely to be impermanent.

There is, however, a more fundamental reason why this approach does not work. We are responding to our mental needs as if they were bodily needs – as if their cause lay in the world around us. While our bodily needs are a symptom of some physical lack – a lack of food or heat – the same is not true of our psychological needs. Most of the time the cause is in our minds. We feel insecure because we imagine misfortunes that might befall us in the future. Or we feel low self-esteem because we tell ourselves that we are not able to live up to some ideal that we have set ourselves. There may well be physical causes for our concern – events may not turn out as we would wish, we may not be achieving our goals – but, as we shall see later, the reason that we feel insecure, unworthy, or whatever, is as much a result of how we interpret and judge events as it is a result of the events themselves.

Most of the time, however, we forget that our inner needs have an inner cause as well as an outer one. We perceive other people or external circumstance to be the root of our discomfort, and respond as we would to a physical lack – by making adjustments to the physical world. But this only deals with part of the problem. The inner lack continues, and soon reappears in some other guise. And so the apparent need continues.

Survival of the Self

The same is true of our need for a sense of self. Most people derive a sense of identity from their experience of and interaction with the world. I 'am' my personality and my character; I am my social status and my job; I am my body and my sex; I am my nationality, my name, my family; I am my beliefs, my education, my interests, my clothes – and even sometimes my car!

Such an identity is forever vulnerable. It has no permanent foundation, so is continually at the mercy of events in the world around. This results in a repeated need to reassert a sense of self and reestablish who we are. This can lead to many unnecessary and often undesirable behaviors. Some worry about how they look. Others feel they must constantly defend their characters. We may feel insulted if someone forgets our name. We may be proud of our education, and like others to be aware of it. Some of us may argue for hours defending our beliefs. Others say things they do not believe in order to be noticed. We may buy expensive or fashionable clothes, not because we need them, but because they have become part of who we are. And, if someone damages our car – or even insults it – we may not always respond as one might expect a rational, intelligent being to respond.

If this were as far as it went, such behavior would be fairly innocuous. But its consequences spread out into our surroundings. Moreover, when augmented by our technology, the repercussions can be very damaging indeed.

The Amplification of Error

Technology amplifies the power inherent in the human hand, and thus amplifies our ability to change the world according to our desires. In the service of our physical needs, this has been of benefit. It gave us plows, irrigation, housing, sanitation, and heating. But in the service of our inner needs it has been far from beneficial. Unconsciously assuming that these needs can also be satisfied by changing the world around – and not being ones to give up easily – we have applied our creative energies and our technologies towards the search for more and more powerful ways of getting what we think we want. But since nothing we have or do ever brings lasting fulfillment of our inner needs, all that technology has amplified is the error in our thinking.

And with potentially disastrous consequences. It is the demands we make of the world in our relentless search for inner fulfillment that lead us to consume far more than we physically need. No other species consumes more than it needs. But no other species has our inner needs, or the means to amplify the demands they give rise to. It is this combination that is causing us to suck the Earth dry.

Our unfulfilled needs for security, power, and approval lead us to make inappropriate political, economic, environmental, and industrial decisions. Overconcerned with our perceived well-being, we disperse toxins we could contain, and carelessly eliminate tens of thousands of other species sharing our planet. And our need to defend our own beliefs turns others into enemies, makes us kill *en masse*, and focuses half our scientific research on national defense.

Seen in this light, the nuclear threat, the greenhouse effect, the destruction of the rainforests, the wide-scale extinction of species, acid rain, soil erosion, the depletion of the ozone layer, the problem of atomic waste, pollution, the energy crisis, the North-South crisis, the economic crisis, the food crisis, the water crisis, the housing crisis, the sanitation crisis, and the many other crises that humanity faces are all symptoms of a deeper psychological crisis.

The real crisis is in our thinking, in our perception of what it is we really want, and how to set about getting it.

How has this come about? Why do we presume that what we have or do will satisfy our inner needs?

HYPNOTIZED –
THE MATERIALIST MINDSET

Society is in conspiracy against the manhood of every
one of its members. Society is a joint-stock company in
which the members agree, for the better securing of his
bread to each shareholder, to surrender the liberty of
the eater.

Ralph Waldo Emerson

One of the reasons we look to the world for the satisfaction of our
inner needs is our past experience. As growing children we found
that we could satisfy our needs for warmth, food, comfort, and
stimulation by influencing the world around us. We discovered the
power of our hands. And, as an evolving culture, we learnt the
power of technology. We experienced how to create many additional tools and facilities by further modifications of our surroundings.

So successful have we become at molding and manipulating the
world, we have come to believe that modifying our surroundings is
the way to solve all our problems – not necessarily the only way, but
the easiest and simplest way.

For reasons we have already touched on, and shall return to later,
this approach does not work so well when it comes to our inner
needs. But seduced by the power of our hands and conditioned by
past experience we still try to satisfy them in the way we know best.
When this fails to bring any real or permanent satisfaction we do
not question whether our approach may be mistaken. Instead we
try harder and harder to get the world to give us what we want. We
buy more clothes, go to more parties, eat more food, try to make
more money. Or we give up on these and try different things. We

take up squash, buy a video camera, decide to move house, or look for new friends. Yet true peace of mind remains as elusive as ever.

We are rather like Nasrudhin, the 'wise-fool' of Sufi tales, who has lost his key somewhere in his house. But he is searching for it out in the street 'because,' he says, 'there is more light outside.' We too look for the key to fulfillment in the world around because that is the world we know best. We know how to change this world, how to gather possessions, how to make people and things behave the way we want – the way we think will bring us happiness. We know much less about our minds and how to find fulfillment within ourselves. There seems to be 'much less light in there.'

A Cultural Trance

Past experience is not the only reason we focus so much of our attention on modifying the world around us. From the moment we are born our culture encourages us to believe that outer well-being is the source of inner fulfillment.

As young children we learn from the example of our elders that it is important to be in control of things, that material possessions offer security, and that doing and saying the right things is the way to gain another person's love. As we grow up much of our education focuses on knowing the ways of the world in order that we might better manage our affairs and so satisfy both our physical and our psychological needs. And, as we go through life, the daily deluge of television, radio, newspapers, magazines, and billboards reinforces the belief that happiness comes from what happens to us. Wherever we turn the principle is confirmed, encouraging us to become 'human havings' and 'human doings' rather than human beings.

Somewhere deep inside most of us know this way of operating has its limits. We recognize that whether or not we are content depends as much on how we are inside as on how things are around us. We all know people who can remain cheerful when everything seems to be going wrong; who do not get upset at having to wait in a long line or queue – even in the rain. And we hear of more unusual examples – those who have maintained an inner equanimity despite the atrocities of war, or yogis who can apparently sleep peacefully on a bed of nails. The trouble is our cultural hypnosis is so strong that this inner knowing rarely comes to the surface.

Our society has caught itself in a vicious circle. If most of us go through life on the assumption that psychological contentment comes from what we have or do, then that is the message we teach each other. If we see somebody suffering, we are more likely than not to suggest ways they can change the situation so as to feel better. When we want to persuade someone to buy something or other, we tell them how much happier it will make them. And when our best-laid plans fail to give us what we seek, we encourage each other to try again.

It is as if we have all been hypnotized – or, to be more accurate, as if we have all hypnotized each other.

An Exploitative Consciousness

Few of us question the validity of our conditioning. As with classical hypnosis, we put our own knowing to one side and follow other people's suggestions of how we should see reality and how we should behave. We do as everyone else does.

Looking outside ourselves for the fulfillment of our needs may have been of value in the past when physical survival was our prime concern – and it may still be of value when we are hungry or in some other physical need – but the drives that now dominate most of our lives are psychological rather than physical, and this approach seldom brings any true or lasting satisfaction.

Worse, it now threatens our collective survival. Not only does it lead to prolific overconsumption, this way of operating also lies at the heart of our malignant behavior.

One of the most damaging consequences of looking to the world to satisfy our inner needs is a competitive mode of consciousness. Perceiving that our surroundings are limited in what they can provide, we compete for the things we believe will bring us happiness – fame, success, friends, promotion, power, attention, and money. Such competition is wasteful. It leads us to produce things that no one really needs and to do things that are not really necessary. It encourages short cuts in the name of financial expediency. It promotes blinkered thinking and shortsightedness. It causes us to care less for the world than we do for our own well-being. It even puts us in competition with Nature herself – insecticides, herbicides, and fungicides keep other species at bay so that we can more easily, and more profitably, accomplish our own ends.

This basic operating principle also results in an exploitative mode of consciousness. We use – or perhaps one should say 'abuse' – our surroundings, other people, and even our own bodies in our quest for greater satisfaction. This is the root of our exploitation of the world: the attitudes and values that come from believing that inner well-being is dependent upon what we have or do. Money, power, and the other things that people often blame are not the root cause; they are simply symptoms of a deeper underlying error in our thinking.

The Ego-Mode

It is this mode of consciousness that makes humanity so riddled with self-centeredness. We want things for ourselves. We want to be in control of our surroundings. We want to have our own way.

We usually think of egocentricity as the influence of a part of ourselves called the 'ego' – the part that is self-interested and concerned with its own well-being. But we can also see egocentricity as a mode of thinking. It is the mode that stems from the assumption that our happiness depends upon what happens to us. For it is this mindset that causes us to do and say all manner of things in order to manipulate the world – and that includes other people – into giving us what we want.

Thus rather than thinking of our self as being composed of various different parts – which is, after all, something of a contradiction – we can consider the self as a single self that functions in different modes, one of which is the ego-mode. In this respect the ego is not so much a thing as a belief system – albeit a most deeply ingrained one.

The Mind's Bottom Line

Our self-interest is often blamed for the ills of the world. But there is nothing wrong with self-interest as such. As we discussed in the previous chapter, it is perfectly natural to look after one's own well-being and survival. Nor is there anything wrong in seeking happiness for ourselves. To move away from pain and suffering towards greater contentment is the intrinsic nature of consciousness. It is the mind's fundamental goal.

I may decide to change jobs because I believe I will be happier. I may choose to play table tennis with a friend because I expect to get some pleasure from the game, some good feelings from the exercise, and some satisfaction from winning – or perhaps from seeing my friend win. I may take up hang-gliding because I find the challenge enjoyable – or because I get a kick from the release of adrenalin. I may spend time writing a book, foregoing other pleasures, because I gain satisfaction from following my inner drive. If my mind wanders into daydreams, it is probably because they are more entertaining than the task at hand. And I may meditate to be at peace within myself.

This does not mean that our search is always successful. Sometimes, through shortsightedness or factors beyond our control, we do not achieve our objectives. At other times we may well get the things we desire only to find they have not made us any happier; they may even have led us to suffer more. How many people have started a new job, a new course of study, or a new relationship, believing it will make them happy, only to discover later they were happier the way things were?

Nor is it always immediate gratification that we are after. We may not enjoy visiting the dentist, but we go in order that life be more enjoyable later. At other times we may worry about the future, creating much discomfort for ourselves, because we unconsciously assume that our worrying will help us avoid future sources of discomfort.

The same principle lies behind our more altruistic actions. We may give up all sense of personal gain and devote time to helping others feel better, perhaps putting ourselves to considerable inconvenience or hardship. But we do it because at some deeper level we feel better for it.

Even the masochist who sets out to cause himself pain does so because he gets pleasure from it – or imagines he will.

A happier state of consciousness is the mind's bottom line. It is the fundamental criterion by which, consciously or unconsciously, we make our decisions.

Trying to discourage this drive is to miss the point of life. Our error lies not in the seeking of a more enjoyable inner state, but in the ways we seek it. Our cultural conditioning has trapped us in a materialist mindset – a belief system that says if we are not happy then something in the world of matter needs to change.

This is the 'virus' that has infected our minds. This is the bug in our thinking – the bug that lies at the root of our malignant attitudes and behaviors. For it is this redundant assumption that underlies so much of our greed. It is the reason why we have become so addicted to what we have and what we do.

Addicted to the Material World

Normally we think of addiction in terms of drugs, but the effects of our materialist mindset bear all the hallmarks of chemical dependency. Whatever the drug – whether it be alcohol, tobacco, coffee, tranquilizers, or some illicit substance – people take it for one simple reason: they want to feel better. They want to feel happy, high, relaxed, in control, free from fear, more in touch with life. In this respect the drug-taker is seeking nothing different from anyone else – it is just the way in which he or she is doing it that contemporary society finds unacceptable.

It is the same with our addiction to materialism. We are trying to make ourselves feel better. But any happiness we get is usually only temporary; as soon as one 'high' wears off we go in search of another 'fix.' We become psychologically dependent on our favorite sources of pleasure – sex, food, rock'n'roll, driving, debating, football, fighting, television – whatever it is we get off on. (Or whatever it is we believe we should get off on.) And the ever-present problem of habituation means we need larger and larger doses to achieve the same effect.

This is our most dangerous addiction – our addiction to things. For it is this addiction that underlies the materialism of our age. And nowhere is this addiction more apparent than in our addiction to money.

MONEY –
THE ROOT OF ALL EVIL?

All the money in the world is spent on feeling good.

Ry Cooder

We can now begin to understand why people value money so much. Money gives us the means to obtain the things or situations we desire. It allows us to buy food, clothing, shelter, heating and other physical necessities. But more importantly, in terms of our psychological dependence, it allows us to buy the goods and services we think will make our future more secure, give us greater control over our world, bring us recognition and approval from others, keep us entertained, and reinforce our sense of identity. With money we can buy whatever it is we believe will take us towards a happier state of mind.

But so useful is money in helping us get the things we desire that some of us seem to have forgotten what it is we are really after. Many behave as if money itself were the ultimate bottom line. For them, simply having money becomes a source of security, recognition, power, and identity. Self-worth and financial worth become indistinguishable.

In today's world those with money are often regarded as the 'lucky ones.' Most of those 'less fortunate' wish that they too could have more money. Then, so they tell themselves, all their problems would be solved.

As a result many of us are continually on the lookout for the best buy, the best deal, the best wage, the best return on our investment. The implicit assumption is that the more money we have, the happier we will be.

I will not go into the the rights or wrongs of particular economic systems. Nor will I explore the reality or otherwise of money, the nature of credit, the arcane mysteries of the world banking system, or the questionable morality of usury. Many far more qualified than I have already dealt with such issues at considerable length – and will doubtless continue to do so.

Suffice it to say, that most of us have got ourselves well and truly caught by money.

Adding Fuel to the Fire

It does not take a great mind to see that financial expediency lies behind many of our short-sighted decisions, much of our inhumanity to each other, our callous treatment of other creatures, and our cavalier attitude towards our surroundings. How many times have we heard it said that preventing a certain type of pollution would cost too much? Why else would we leave grain mountains sitting in one country while a few thousand miles away millions starve to death?

There are other ways, too, in which our attachment to money exacerbates the global crisis. Economic theory tells us that a growing economy is a healthy one. To an extent that may be true; economic growth means increased products and services and in most cases a higher standard of living. But few people pause to ask whether we in the West really need to improve our standard of living yet further. We remain wedded to the notion of economic growth – and the faster our economies grow, the more we consume and the more waste we produce.

Nor should we ignore the likely impact of Third World countries struggling hard to catch up and attain similar standards to those that we enjoy. Their need for growth, it could be argued, is much more urgent than ours. But at what cost? It inevitably increases both consumption of resources and the production of waste, adding further fuel to the global fire.

In addition, most of these poorer countries have taken out large loans in order to finance their development. Many now find themselves unable to generate sufficient additional wealth to repay the interest on their loans – let alone the loans themselves – and are forced to sell their natural assets to the highest bidder.

As a result rainforests are consumed even faster. Species become extinct more rapidly than we can classify them as endangered. More and more of the Earth is torn up to meet the ever-growing demand for raw materials. And the extra waste generated by all this additional industrial activity fouls the air, pollutes the water, and poisons the land.

And we continue to be told that sustained economic growth is healthy. Healthy for whom?

Preying on Illusions

Since the majority of us in the First World already have most of the things we need for our physical well-being, the only way our economies can continue to grow is to turn to the satisfaction of our psychological needs.

The fact that material goods can never really satiate these needs has to be kept quiet. Instead an artificial sense of scarcity must be created. We have to be convinced that we are not fulfilled as we are. That we cannot be content with what we have. We must be persuaded that wearing the latest jeans will make us feel better. Smoking a specific brand of cigarette will add to our image. Saving with a particular bank will bring us greater security. Buying a new car will make our lives more comfortable. Eating in a certain restaurant will bring us greater satisfaction. And so on.

However, before we blame the 'system' let us remember that for such persuasion to work we have first to fall for it. And we fall for it because we remain under the illusion that our inner needs can be satisfied by what we have or do. We seldom stop to ask: Will I really be any happier for buying this new article? Instead we go along with the seduction.

We are perpetrators of the system as much as we are its victims.

The Arch-Hypnotist

The last thing our present economic system wishes to see happen is that we wake up and realize that we do not really need most of what we buy. It does not want us to realize that there are better routes to inner satisfaction than continual consumption. This would remove the motor from the economy.

Could this be one reason why our materialist culture seems unwilling to take spiritual development seriously? Does it suspect, perhaps unconsciously, that if we became less attached to the material world, less addicted to what we have and do, our economic system would be thrown into disarray?

The system that raised us out of poverty, physical suffering, and hardship is suddenly saying 'Stop.' It now blocks the path to further liberation, telling us that 'This is all there is.' And that 'Material progress is the best path to inner peace.'

It cannot afford for us to see the limitations of our redundant mindset. Instead it has to keep us convinced that if only we had a little more of what it has to offer we would come closer to inner fulfillment.

Society is caught in a vicious circle. Our assumption that material well-being is the path to inner well-being underlies our love of money. And our love of money leads to an economic system that must maintain this illusion. It has to ensure that we remain in our state of trance.

In other words, our current economic system may well be the most pervasive and persuasive of all our cultural hypnotists.

Breaking the Circle

Somehow this vicious circle has to be broken. But we have to break it at its source.

A doctor seldom heals a patient by simply patching up the symptoms. If he does not look to the underlying cause the problem will more than likely reappear at some later time or in some other guise. Similarly we will not cure the ills of the world by introducing new economic models. They only suppress the symptoms of our malaise. The root of the problem – our attachment to things – will persist, and with it the desire for money to buy these things. Corruption will continue, and those who can will gather and hoard what they may – as evidenced by the Swiss bank accounts of many a fallen leader, of whatever political persuasion.

Nor should we try to eliminate money from our society, as some more radical thinkers have proposed. Some symbolic means of exchange is essential – I may not always want to receive chickens in return for my solar panels.

It is not 'money' that is the root of all evil – as is commonly misquoted – but 'the love of money.' And our love of money is itself but a symptom of a deeper error – our addiction to the world of things.

If we are to move beyond this materialist phase of our evolution, it is to this root of our malaise that we must give our attention.

To see what this entails and where it might lead, we need first to look at some of the effects of this outdated mode of operating on our personal lives. For it is in our personal lives that we will begin to find the keys to change.

FEAR – ATTACHMENT TO TIME

All my possessions for a moment of time.

Queen Elizabeth I, with her dying breath

Looking to the material world for the satisfaction of our inner needs is the source of much fear. All fear is, in essence, fear of the future. We are afraid of things that have not yet happened, but which if they did might bring us pain, suffering, or some other discomfort – or stand in the way of some future contentment. And we are afraid that circumstances that are already causing us displeasure may continue in the future.

Fear is intended to have a positive function. It helps us avoid danger. This is fine as far as our physical survival is concerned. But as human beings we also have various needs for psychological survival. And, caught in our materialist conditioning, we find ourselves fearing anything in the outer world that appears to threaten our inner well-being.

We may fear losing our jobs because of the loss of income and the fear that we might not be able to live so comfortably. We may fear failure for the disapproval it might bring or for the loss of self-esteem. We may fear having nothing to do because we might get bored. We may fear telling the truth because others might not like us for it. We fear the unknown for the dangers it may contain. We fear uncertainty, not knowing whether or not we will find what we are after.

Here lies a sad irony. In the final analysis what we are all after is a more satisfying state of mind. We want to be happy, at peace within ourselves. Our fears stem from the possibility that the future may bring us greater suffering rather than happiness. Yet the very nature of fear makes us more anxious in the present. And a mind that is anxious is not a mind that is at peace.

We have lost the very thing we seek.

The Voice in Our Heads

Many of our fears are not so strong that we would label them as fears. They may just be concerns, little niggles we have about how things might turn out. They may not even be conscious concerns – in many cases they surface only in our dreams, in conversation with a friend, or after a couple of drinks.

Nevertheless, however intense or mild they might be, they fill our minds with thoughts. This is our self-talk, the mental chatter we carry on with ourselves. This is the voice inside our heads that comments, often critically, on everything we do. It thinks, 'I did that well, people will approve of me.' Or it admonishes us, saying, 'If only that had not happened, if only I had said it differently, things would have turned out better.'

It is the voice that speculates on the future. It thinks, 'What if such-and-such were to happen, would it be good for me?' Or 'What if I do this, will it make me more comfortable?' 'Should I make that telephone call . . . just in case?' It wonders what other people are thinking, and how they will react. It wonders what might happen to the economy, to housing prices, to our partner, to our lifestyle, to our image, to our car. It worries, 'Have I made the right decision?' 'Will I have enough money?' 'Will I be able to cope?'

This is the voice of fear.

The voice in our heads believes its function is to guide us towards greater happiness. But it is the voice of the ego-mind – the part of us that believes that only through what happens to us in the world around can we be at peace within. And since the world around seldom brings any lasting satisfaction, the ego-mind is always finding more possibilities to fear, new reasons to be anxious.

This is not to imply that we should not think about the future and not make plans. Our ability to look ahead and gauge the outcome of our actions is one of our most valuable assets. What we do not need is to fill our minds with worry over what might or might not happen. This is not the most constructive use of our imagination, or of our intelligence.

Not Now

Besides giving rise to much unnecessary fear, this internal dialogue keeps us trapped in time. It dwells on the past and future. And as long as we are listening to this mental chatter our attention too is in the past or future. We are not experiencing things as they are, we are seeing them through our judgments of the past and fears for the future.

At times we can be so caught up in our self-talk we do not even notice the present. We do not notice what is going on around us, do not really hear what other people are saying, do not appreciate how we actually feel. So engrossed are we in our concerns we never seem to pause to let things be.

We have lost the present moment. Lost the 'now.'

Saving Time

Similar fears underlie our concern for saving time. We fear that we will not have time to do all the things we think we should if we are to be content.

So we try to do everything as quickly and efficiently as possible, reducing 'unproductive' times such as traveling and shopping to a minimum. Then, so we tell ourselves, we will have more time to spend – to spend, that is, on chasing after fulfillment. Time to experience the world in new ways. Time to explore new interests. Time to earn more money, and buy more of the things we think we need.

Little wonder, then, that time is so often equated with money. We apply the same materialist mindset to both. We tell ourselves that the more time we have at our disposal, the more opportunity we will have of finding greater happiness. But again we are looking to the future, to the times we will create. Again we miss the enjoyment of the present moment.

Fear of the End

The fear of not having enough time is one of the reasons we are so afraid of death. With the end of our bodies comes the end of our eyes and ears onto the world – the end of our experience of the world. All those investments in a worldly future abruptly come to nought. Those pleasures still unenjoyed will remain so.

Death also signifies an end to our doing. An end to all those opportunities to achieve something. What is still undone or unpossessed will remain so. No more will there be the chance to shape the world according to our desires. All those ambitions will remain unachieved. The ego-mind will be able to have its way no longer.

Worse still, the ego-mind will cease to exist. All those aspects of our identity that are derived in one way or another from our interaction with the world will come to an abrupt halt. This self, this unique human being that we think we are, will be finished.

For many this is the greatest fear. The fear of loss of all identity, all consciousness, and all being. The fear of dissolving into nothingness. The fear of an end to our time.

Fear of Each Other

Fear also plays havoc with our relationships. We fear our partners may cease to like us. We fear they may not understand us. We fear being criticized and judged. We fear telling the truth because we fear our partners may react in ways we do not like. We fear rejection. We fear that if they knew what we were really like inside they would not want to be with us. We fear they will not listen to our opinions. We fear they may not be there when we need them. We fear they may prevent us from doing what we want. We fear they might threaten our sense of identity.

And how do we react? We may not express how we really feel. We may hide our true selves. We may manipulate our partners to behave in the way we want. We may make them wrong, blaming them for our fears. We may be more concerned with proving we are right than discovering the truth. We may not listen to them fully. As soon as they say something that goes against one of our own cherished beliefs, the voice in our head tells us where they are wrong and how we should respond – and as long as we are listening to our own self-talk we are not really listening to them. We may attack them in various subtle, or not so subtle, ways, looking for ways to make them fear us.

Then we wonder why our relationships can be so full of tensions and problems.

Nor is it just our intimate relationships that suffer. We find things to fear in our friends, our neighbors, our colleagues and our bosses. We even find things to fear in people we have never met, or may never meet again. Will they make me look foolish? Will I be respected and valued? Will they impose upon me? Will they ignore me?

Fear also disturbs our international relations. We are afraid of different political systems. We are alarmed by other nations' economic dominance. We are frightened by their instability. We dread their military might.

Then, as if there were not sufficient fear in the world, we try to diminish our own fear by having them fear us. And so the vicious circle grows and continues.

Resisting Change

Fear of the future is the primary reason we resist change. Change can threaten our careers, threaten our relationships, threaten our position, threaten our sense of control, threaten our feelings of security, or threaten our freedom. If this is the way we see change then quite naturally we resist it. We resist new technologies, new working practices, new customs, new ways of thinking. We resist changes to our plans, changes in our circumstances, and changes in our lifestyle.

Tragically, we also resist the very changes that we most need to make if we are to survive. We resist giving up our cars, reducing our energy consumption, saving water, recycling our waste, and doing without many of the luxuries to which some of us have become accustomed. Stuck with our material addictions, we anticipate that in some way or another the inconveniences of such changes will cause us some displeasure.

The same pattern underlies our resistance to change on a global level. This is why farmers continue to degrade the soil. Why corporations continue to buy hardwood from the rainforest. Why industries continue to pollute the air and water.

This is why the world continues to spend $750,000,000,000 a year on armaments, rather than on food, sanitation, housing, and education. Someone, somewhere believes the change would not be in their own best interest.

Yet, much as we may resist change, we cannot prevent it. If the patterns of the past hold up – and there is every reason to expect they will – change is going to come faster and faster. We will need to become more flexible, more free in ourselves to accept change. This will require that we let go of our many unnecessary fears.

If we do not then we may well find that fear will be our ruin. For there is one more problem that results from fear – one which we must attend to if we are to survive an ever-accelerating pace of change.

STRESS – THE WAGES OF FEAR

People are disturbed, not by things, but by the view
they take of them.

Epictetus

As far as the body is concerned, fear is a danger signal. And it
responds with an automatic reaction called 'The Flight/Fight
Response.' The heart rate quickens, blood pressure rises, breathing
increases, muscles become tense, the skin begins to sweat, while
digestion, reproduction, and other processes that will not be
needed for the moment are turned down. The body is preparing for
instant action – to flee or to fight.

Such a response is very natural – and is to be found in all animals.
It is also a very valuable response. After all, if you were confronted
by a wild boar in the woods, or were about to be hit by a bus, you
would need to move instantly, and fast.

In contemporary society such physical threats are few and far
between. Our mastery of the world has enabled us to avoid or
guard against most such dangers, and there are seldom times when
we need to prepare ourselves for such instant action. But this does
not mean that we are free from threat. As we have seen, human
beings have created a whole new set of things to worry about.

Our need to feel in control may be threatened by imposed
workloads, tight deadlines, crowded schedules. We may feel
threatened by traffic jams, delayed flights, incompetent staff, unexpected demands, and anything else that might cost us time. Our
need for self-esteem, recognition, and approval can be threatened
by the fear of failure, the fear of looking foolish in front of others,
the fear of criticism, and the fear of being rejected. Uncertainty or

anything else that makes us feel insecure can likewise be perceived as a threat.

Such threats are new to Nature. They are not threats a cat or a dog might feel. They do not have these psychological needs and do not know these fears. We can imagine – and thus worry about – things that a cat or dog could not even conceive of.

The trouble is, our biological evolution has not caught up with our inner evolution. Our bodies respond to these psychological threats just as they would to any physical threat. So we find our hearts thumping, our palms sweating, and our muscles tightening, not because of any physical danger, but because of some danger we perceive within our minds – because someone criticizes us, because we have to speak in a group, or because we may be late for a meeting.

The Toll of Stress

Rarely do these psychological threats demand that we run for our lives or fight to the death. There has been no physical danger. As far as the body is concerned it was all a false alarm. So our physiological system then sets about unwinding and recovering. But this is a much slower process – it takes only a second for the body to jump to alert, but it can take many minutes, sometimes even hours, for it to return to a state of ease.

If this occurred only occasionally there would be no problem. But most of us encounter such inner threats several times a day – sometimes several times an hour – and the body seldom has time to recover from one false alarm before the next one is triggered. Before long our bodies end up in a permanent state of tension – a permanent state of emergency.

For many of us this underlying tension is so much a part of contemporary life that we no longer notice it or pay it much attention. But it is still present – a faint background of uptightness, interspersed with periods of high anxiety. Only when we relax fully do we realize just how tense we normally are.

Over a period of time, this background tension begins to affect our thinking, emotions, and behavior. Our judgment deteriorates; we tend to make more mistakes; our perception becomes poorer; we may become depressed, feel hostile towards others, lose our temper more, act less rationally, behave abusively.

Meanwhile the toll on our bodies manifests in various ways: aches and pains, indigestion, insomnia, high blood pressure, allergies, lowered immunity, illness – sometimes premature death.

And the damage does not end there. Increased tension, friction, anger, hostility, intolerance, anxiety, depression, irrationality, fear, fragility, instability, ineffectiveness and muddled thinking, selfishness and general craziness, all affect the general health and well-being of society. This contributes to increasing crime, vandalism, violence, terrorism (sanctioned as well as unsanctioned), militarization, war, drug abuse (legal as well as illegal), police harassment, divorce . . . and on and on.

Stress can also have negative consequences on our environment. Eighty percent of accidents are caused by 'human error' – and the more stressed a person is, the more prone they are to error. And the consequences of human error in a nuclear power station, a chemical plant, or a tanker full of crude oil are familiar to us all.

Nor do fatigued and tense people always make the best decisions. More often than not stress makes us feel more vulnerable, more in need of defending our own interests, more caught up in our ego-mind.

Stress exacerbates the inner sickness of our time, and in so doing exacerbates the global crisis we have brought upon ourselves.

Fear, once our greatest ally, has become our greatest enemy.

A Disease of the Future

The problem of stress is not likely to go away. As the pace of change continues to increase, the demands upon us will also increase, and the disease of stress will become more and more of a problem. We will find ourselves becoming more tired, making more mistakes, becoming more hostile, more anxious, more depressed, suffering more ill-health, and having more accidents.

If we are to survive in a world of ever-accelerating change, it is imperative that we learn to cope with the increasing pressures without accumulating yet more tension and all its unwanted effects. If we do not, it is more than probable that we will find ourselves sucked into a downward spiral, desperately trying to manage in an increasingly unmanageable world. Breakdowns and burnouts will become the norm. And society will head yet faster towards its own collapse.

The Inner Dimension

Because we are caught in the belief that our inner state is at the mercy of external events, we usually try to manage stress by managing the world. We seek to eliminate or reduce the circumstances that we think are the cause of our stress. And we seek to minimize the effects that these stresses have on our body and behavior – by, for example, giving the body the rest it needs to recover.

While these may be helpful courses of action it is also becoming clear that the mind plays a crucial role in most stress reactions. I may, for example, think that being stuck in a traffic jam causes me stress. In doing so I overlook the crucial role that my own thinking plays in my reaction. It is not the traffic jam itself that is causing the tension. A traffic jam is actually quite relaxing. No activity is called for, no vigilance is required, there is nothing that needs to be controlled, nobody coming along to interrupt my thoughts. In many respects it is the sort of situation I may have been wishing for all day. I can shut my eyes and come to no harm.

If I find such a situation stressful it is because of what I am telling myself – that voice in the head again. I may be imagining the possible negative consequences of being delayed, or be angry with myself for not having chosen a better route. I may be saying that this is not what I expected; I want the situation to be different from the way it is. It is my thoughts that make me upset, not the jam itself.

Someone else who remains relaxed in a jam may be glad to be away from the demands of telephones, papers to sign, questions to answer, disagreements to settle. One may be pleased to have to miss the meeting. Or one may realize that there is nothing that can be done to change the situation, so may as well arrive late and relaxed as late and upset.

In most cases it is not the situation itself that causes stress but the way in which we perceive the situation. If I see the situation as a threat to what I want, a threat to my sense of identity, a threat to my inner well-being, a threat to my getting what I believe I need in order to be happy, or a threat to my expectations of how things should be, then I may well cause myself stress.

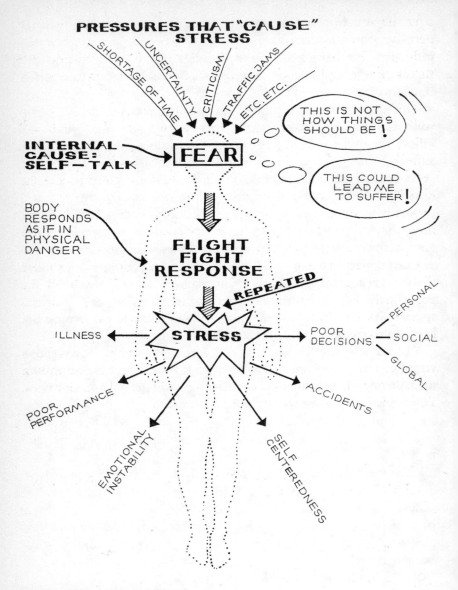

Managing the Mind

The fact that it is our perception of events as much as, if not more than, the events themselves that trigger our reactions suggests that we can have far more influence over our responses than we normally realize.

By taking responsibility for our own inner processes we can put ourselves back in control. We may not always have much influence over the situation we find ourselves in, but the way in which we perceive a situation is something over which we have a great deal of influence. We have a choice as to whether we see a change as a threat or as an opportunity. And so we have a choice as to whether or not we upset ourselves over things.

This does not mean that we should sit back and let the world walk all over us. There may be many things we can do that will relieve the pressure we are under. If, for instance, we find ourselves suffering from an excessive workload, we can look for ways to reduce that particular problem. What we do not need to do is make ourselves upset, and possibly ill, in the process. In fact we will probably respond with more insight, higher creativity, clearer direction, better poise, and more effectiveness, if our minds are not hampered by a response more appropriate to our evolutionary past.

Learning to manage your own thinking and perception is more than a very practical means of managing stress – with all the consequent benefits that may have on us as individuals and as a species. As you learn to work with yourself in this way, you are learning to free yourself from fear.

You are learning to deal with the source of all fear – the voice in your head that judges and interprets what it sees. You are beginning to challenge the fundamental operating principle that runs our lives. You are learning to leave the ego-mind behind.

DREAMING –
A SELF HALF-AWAKE

Deep within the human soul lies an unfamiliar force
which is stronger than all the external forces that
surround us. The force is unfamiliar because we have
forgotten what it sounds like and what it needs to
release it.

H.R.H. The Prince of Wales

'How is it that human beings can be so intelligent and at the same
time so stupid?' That was the question that started our exploration
into the human mind. Part of the answer, we have seen, lies in our
attempt to fulfill our various inner mental needs as if they were
material needs – we try to change the world rather than change our
minds. This fallacious assumption lies at the root of much of our
craziness.

Somewhat paradoxically, this error stems from the very factors
that make us so intelligent. As well as experiencing the world
through our senses, we can also think about what we see and hear,
form concepts, and make generalizations. We can study the structure of the material world and understand the laws that govern it.
As a result our consciousness of the world has been greatly
expanded.

But we have not awoken to the inner world of mind to a similar
extent. This world is less concrete than the physical world. Our eyes
and ears cannot perceive it, nor can words so readily label and
describe it. Our knowledge of our subconscious realms is still very
scant. We do not understand how we come to think as we do. We
are not fully aware of our inner needs and deeper motivations, nor
of what influences our perception. Many of us find it difficult to

describe our emotions. And nearly all of us have trouble defining that most essential part of us: our self.

Nor are we able to exercise much influence over our internal states. Our hands cannot reach in and change our minds. When we try to 'manipulate' our inner world most of us turn to some physical means – to diet, exercise, drugs, or some other process or product that affects the functioning of our brains. Managing the mind directly is – in contemporary Western culture at least – much less common.

In short we are only conscious of half of reality – and, some would argue, the lesser half at that. We are, by and large, still asleep to the realm of mind.

A Waking Dream

The notion that we are half-asleep is common to many philosophies and spiritual teachings. The Russian mystic, G.I. Gurdjieff, for example, claimed that most of us live in a waking trance. He argued that we function like machines, along lines of fixed habit. We may think we are acting freely, consciously, and intelligently, but much of the time we 'run on automatic,' not actually choosing our responses.

How many of us have not at some time had a second helping of some tasty dish, and then consumed it 'on automatic,' only to realize later that we did not really taste it – and perhaps did not even really want it?

In many respects we live as in a dream. Our concerns for what might or might not happen color our perceptions of the world, often leading us to see things very differently from how they really are. Indian teachings sometimes use the example of a man who, walking in the dusk, comes across a piece of rope lying on the ground. In the half-light he sees it as a snake, and goes running back to his village shouting 'Snake! Snake!' Only when he returns with a light does he see it is a rope, and realize that all his fears were groundless. In our semi-wakeful state of consciousness our hidden fears may give rise to many similar waking dreams.

Although dreams may exist only in our imagination, they can nevertheless seem as real as our waking experience. Take a type of nighttime dream that many of us have had – that of being chased by people intent on causing us harm. As long as we are dreaming there is no question that the threat is real, and our bodies react accordingly. We have all awoken from such nightmares to find our hearts pounding and our bodies bathed in sweat. Only as full wakefulness returns do we realize that it was all 'only a dream.'

'Real life' can be very similar. We may, for instance, think that another person is attacking us in some way – criticizing us perhaps. We may react by becoming tense, by trying to defend ourselves, or possibly by returning the attack. Only later may we discover that we had completely misinterpreted the situation and that this person was really trying to be helpful. Once again it had all been a dream.

According to the Buddha – and to many other teachers – such waking dreams lie at the root of our suffering. To the extent that we are caught up in our dreams, such suffering is very real. This is the first 'noble truth' of Buddhism. The second is that suffering is self-created; it is the result of our craving for pleasure in the world. The third is the recognition that this is unnecessary; the recognition that we are living in a dream. And the fourth is the 'eightfold way' by which we can awaken from this dream and so end our suffering.

Before we can even begin to set about waking up, however, we have first to realize that most of what we fear is only an illusion. But we have become so seduced by the 'reality' of the material world that most of us not only believe our dreams are real, we also believe that we are what we dream we are – a body that moves through places and events. As a result our bodies have become the central figure in our waking dreams – a point brought out clearly by the contemporary spiritual text, *A Course in Miracles:*

> It puts things on itself that it has bought with little metal discs or paper strips the world proclaims as valuable and real. It works to get them, doing senseless things, and tosses them away for senseless things it does not need and does not even want. It hires other bodies, that they may protect it and collect more senseless things that it can call its own. It looks about for special bodies that can share its dream. Sometimes it dreams it is a conqueror of bodies weaker than itself. But in some phases of the dream, it is the slave of bodies that would hurt and torture it.

All the time that we remain caught in our dreams, we see ourselves as bodies at the mercy of the world. We remain only dimly aware of the other half of our reality – the dreamer of the dream.

SELF – THE DREAMER OF THE DREAM

What is the Self?
Neti, Neti – not this, not that.

The Brihadaranyaka Upanishad

Language may have given us the ability to describe and define our experience, but it is not very helpful when we try to describe or define our own self, the 'I' that is experiencing.

Trying to describe the self is rather like setting out with a torch to search for the source of the torch's light. All I would find as I shone the torch around would be the various objects that the light fell upon. However hard I looked I would not locate the source of light. It is the same when I try to discover the nature of 'I.' All that I am aware of are various aspects of my self that the light of consciousness happens to fall upon – my personality, character, memories, ambitions, habits, beliefs, feelings, intelligence, failings, and so on. Try as I may, I cannot find the source of that light. I cannot find the source of my own experience, the unchanging, permanent core of my being.

Some philosophies have concluded that there is no such thing as an independent self. In a sense they are correct. The experiencer is not a *thing* to be experienced. It is more correctly a *no-thing*. In this respect it is indeed nothing.

I Am the Truth

This does not mean that we, as conscious experiencing beings, do not exist. That much is undeniable. We may question the truth of what we think, and we may question the reality of what we experience through the senses. But what we cannot question is the fact that we think and that we experience.

This is what Descartes was saying in his famous phrase, 'Cogito ergo sum' – 'I think therefore I am.' It was not, as is often interpreted, that his thinking was the *cause* of his existence. On the contrary, it was a symptom of his existence – and proof of his existence.

Descartes was searching for the absolute truth – for that which is beyond all doubt. He found that, although he could doubt the content of any thought that he might have, he could not doubt the fact that he thought. And thus he could not doubt his own existence.

Consciousness itself cannot be denied. It is the truth. Your being is the truth. You *are* the truth.

The Self-Existent One

Consciousness is by definition 'that with which we know' – from the Latin *con-scire* – the ultimate prerequisite for all knowing. As such it is as essential for experience as air is for sound or light for sight.

Yet, by virtue of the fact that it is 'that with which we know,' it cannot be known in the way that things are known – as an object of experience. All that we can say is: 'Consciousness is.' Period.

It is self-existent. It cannot be qualified.

Nor does it need any qualification. We all know what it is. Each of us knows what it means to be conscious.

However, because our familiarity with the world around us is considerably more developed than our familiarity with the realm of mind, we do not yet fully appreciate that consciousness itself is the 'I' that we seek to know. In our half-awakened state it is easy to overlook our own essence and identify instead with our more tangible aspects – with our physical form, our personality, our profession, our position, our past, our potential, and so on.

Such attributes are conditioned by events and can change with time. They are not a single, permanent, unchanging, independent self. They are part of our dream, not the dreamer itself.

To realize the nature of consciousness itself has been an eternal quest of humanity. It was this call that was inscribed above the portals of the ancient Greek oracle at Delphi, *Gnothi Seauton* – 'Know thyself.' And in one way or another it is the core of most of the major world religions. Knowing our own inner being releases us from the grip of the ego-mind. Only then can we become fully conscious and see the world as it is. Only then can we become fully mature human beings.

In the past such self-realization has been the privilege of a fortunate few. But the ravages of our self-centeredness upon the world now make such an awakening essential to the salvation of our species. It needs to become the norm rather than the exception.

MATURITY –
COMING OF AGE

The distance between man and the gods is not all that
much greater than the distance between beasts and
man. We have already closed the latter gap, and there is
no reason to suppose that we shall not eventually close
the former.

Ken Wilber

Our state of semi-awakening is not something we are stuck with. It
is just a reflection of our as yet incomplete inner development, both
as individuals and as a species.

It has long been recognized that from the moment of conception
our biological development mirrors the evolution of our species.
Like the first life on Earth, our own life starts as a single cell. This
cell divides, becoming a simple colony, and folds in upon itself to
form a simple tube – much as early multicellular organisms started
off as simple 'feeding tubes.' After a few weeks the growing embryo
develops gills as if it were becoming a fish. Then it resembles a
reptile and a little later takes on some of the characteristics of
smaller mammals. Even at week ten it still has a tail.

Scientists sum up these parallels in the phrase 'ontogeny recapitu-
lates phylogeny.' Translated into simpler English that means 'the
development of the individual (ontogeny) is a summary of the
development of the species (phylogeny).'

Although the principle is usually applied only to our biological
development, similar patterns can be seen in our psychological
development. The stages that our species went through in the
evolution of its consciousness are paralleled in the newborn human
being as it embarks upon its own journey of inner development.

A year or so into life we start to walk – something our hominid ancestors did several million years ago. During our second year we learn to use words; and later we begin to entertain ideas and make abstractions – developments that parallel the evolution of language and thought.

As we grow so does our awareness. To begin with we are learning how to interpret the data pouring in through our senses and how to control our bodies. At this stage there is little distinction between self and surroundings. A sense of individuality begins to dawn only as we move from total dependence upon our mothers towards greater autonomy. We learn how to use our hands and how to create change in the world. We discover relationships of cause and effect, and develop a will. Through this growing interaction with the world comes the realization that we are independent entities – people in our own right. And as our facility with language develops we begin to give expression to this realization. 'I like this.' 'I want that.' 'I can do this.'

These steps in inner development would seem to mirror the stages that early humanity passed through. To begin with, the general consciousness was probably similar to that of a young baby – people were aware of the world and aware of themselves as physical beings but had little sense of an individual self. If there was any sense of identity it was of oneness with the Great Mother – Nature, the provider of all.

It was the development of tools and the move away from an agrarian culture towards civilization that sowed the seeds for the emergence of a more egoic consciousness. We discovered our ability to change the world, to influence the behavior of the Great Mother. We were something special – separate, independent beings with a will of our own. A new sense of identity had been born.

The Descent into Matter

One almost universal characteristic of young children is their purity. What parent has not looked at her young child and marveled at the light that shines through him? Children have an innocence that adults have lost, an awareness of simple truths that we have forgotten. They are reminders of how we too once were.

This purity seems to be something innate. Children do not learn it from their parents – on the contrary, parents frequently find their children to be the teachers in these matters. Nor is it something they are educated into – if anything they are educated out of it.

More likely it is a reflection of human consciousness in its natural, unsullied state.

It is the same with the development of our species. What evidence we have of life in early communities suggests a much greater concern with spiritual issues than is found in modern civilization. Our ancestors seemed to have both awe and reverence for the mysteries of Nature.

Archaeological artifacts are not the only evidence we have for how our forebears might have lived. There are many contemporary examples of so-called 'primitive' cultures – the Kogi of Colombia, the Yanomami of Brazil, the Bushmen of the Kalahari – that remain untainted by the materialism of Western civilization. They know many simple truths that we appear to have forgotten. They smile at our attachment to things, and the energy we put into trying to be masters of our world. They have a deep respect for their local ecology; they know how to live in harmony with the land and other living beings. And, like little children, they can be teachers to us, reminding us of the innocence we have lost in the rush of progress. And of the wisdom that we are now seeking to regain.

This loss of purity – both in the growing child and in a technological society – is probably unavoidable. It is part of the process of development, part of our engagement with the world of matter. The more a child learns how to control the world the more fascinated he becomes with his discoveries – with what he can do and with what he can achieve.

Likewise with our social development. As our tools became more powerful and our understanding of the world deepened, we became fascinated by the changes we could create. Our urge to improve the quality of life led to the Industrial Revolution. And its successes reinforced our infatuation with the material world.

The more ways we discovered to manipulate and change the world, the more our belief that we were individuals in control of our own destiny was strengthened. As our abilities grew we seduced ourselves into believing that such prowess could satisfy all our needs, psychological as well as physical.

This preoccupation with our own well-being led us to become increasingly self-centered. More and more we saw ourselves as separate individuals, each concerned with his or her own fulfill-ment, competing with others for the means to achieve it – and with all the dangers that that entails. Less and less were we prepared to devote ourselves to the group – indeed, the more industrialized we became, the more self-interest became a virtue.

This sense of separateness was further boosted by a scientific paradigm that saw the world as a mechanism, devoid of spirit – even devoid of consciousness. Like a boisterous teenager we became full of ourselves and our capacities, relishing our new-found sense of freedom from the family. Except that in this case the family that had brought us up and supported us so far, and from which we were now separating ourselves, was Mother Earth.

Beyond Temptation

Seduction by the delights and promises of material development is probably a phase that every developing culture must pass through. For various historical and geographic reasons Western Europe may have spearheaded the Industrial Revolution, but other regions such as North America and Australasia quickly followed suit and soon caught up – and in some respects overtook their European cousins.

It hardly needs pointing out that there are still enormous numbers of people in the Third World who do not yet enjoy the same standards as the West. Most are eager to join the party. And who can blame them? Material development offers something they are lacking. Food, fresh water, sanitation, housing. Release from having to toil in fields for twelve hours every day. Improvements in the quality of life. And eventually, they hope, the many comforts and luxuries that we enjoy. They see a more satisfying state and want to move towards it.

Developing countries do not have to start from scratch as Europe did. They do not have to reinvent the steam-engine, the electric motor, the telephone, or the computer. Nor do they have to rediscover systems of mass production, distribution, finance, and marketing. It has already been done. And those who have done it are more than willing to share what they have learned. Positive feedback is at work once again.

As a result, India went through its own Industrial Revolution in only twenty years. China may not even see a true Industrial Age, but may leap from an Agricultural Age into the Information Age. In the case of Japan this has already happened. And several other South-East Asian countries are close on its heels.

Development has now become so fast that most of the other nations may catch up with the First World within another ten or twenty years. Such a possibility fills many minds with trepidation.

How could the planet possibly sustain such a level of growth? It's having problems enough with the West's development. Yet would we want three-quarters of our family to remain stuck in poverty and squalor?*

The question we should be asking is how the rest of our species can enjoy a high standard of living without destroying the world in the process.

Ontogeny Heralds Phylogeny

Important as it is to see our absorption with material things as an unavoidable phase in our development, it is equally important to see it as a passing phase. Most of us do move beyond adolescence. We learn from our experience (to varying degrees). We learn to be less self-centered; we learn to take responsibility.

As we grow older we admit that there is much we do not know and will never know. We become wiser about human nature – its virtues and its failings. We accept the ways of Nature. We become less attached to our possessions; less upset by events of little consequence; less needful of others' appreciation. Many of us become better at living in the present. And some of us come to accept our own mortality.

A few of us may even come to know that we are free, that our well-being is not dependent upon the world we perceive. These enlightened ones may release themselves from all their imagined burdens and find true peace of mind. They may even complete their inner awakening and come to know the nature of consciousness as fully as we now know the world of form. These are the ones we call the saints and mystics – those whose lives have illuminated the history of humanity. The awakened ones.

At the moment full maturity is still a rarity. However, rather than considering such individuals as exceptions we should think of them as heralds. They are portents of what could lie ahead of us as our own inner maturity blossoms. They are also portents of what could lie ahead for the human race – should we survive our troubled adolescence.

In this respect ontogeny *heralds* phylogeny. Both as individuals and as a species we are heading in the direction of self-liberation.

---

* Ultimately we are all cousins – even if seventeen or more times removed.

FREEDOM –
EMANCIPATION FROM MATTER

These things shall be – a loftier race
Than e'er the world hath known shall rise
With flame of freedom in their souls,
And light of knowledge in their eyes.

John Symonds

Both human development and the evolution of life share another significant trend – a journey towards greater freedom from physical constraints.

Some early evolutionary examples are the processes by which living systems obtained energy. The first bacteria used simple fermentation. They broke down sugar molecules into smaller molecules such as carbon dioxide and water, taking for their own use the energy which bound these molecules together.

This process was limited by the availability of these sugars and certain acids, and after a while (a billion years or so) supplies began to run low. Some bacteria escaped from this constraint by developing a new way of obtaining food, photosynthesis. Using the energy of sunlight, they converted carbon dioxide, water, and minerals into energy-rich organic compounds. Since these simpler molecules were much more abundant than the sugars needed for fermentation, the new cells could survive in a greater variety of territories. A new degree of freedom had been established.

But this process had its own drawbacks. It produced oxygen as a waste product. To us oxygen might seem a most beneficial gas, yet it is a very reactive chemical. Combining readily with many other substances, it can destroy many of the complex molecules on which life depends. To the cells of the time it was poisonous pollution.

After several hundred million years so much oxygen had accumulated in the atmosphere that it threatened life on Earth. Nature's response was to exploit oxygen's destructive qualities. Through the process of 'respiration' it found a way of trapping the energy that oxygen released as it reduced (that is, 'burnt') larger molecules into smaller components. This was far more efficient than either fermentation or photosynthesis, and could make use of a much wider range of resources. Organisms were able to feed not only on sugars, minerals, and gases, but also on much more complex organic molecules, on the products of other cells, and even on other organisms. Life had thrown off another major constraint and could now explore a whole new avenue of evolution – the animal kingdom.

The animals that first colonized the land were amphibians. But they could never roam far from water. Even toads, who spend most of their life on land, have to return to water in order to reproduce, since tadpoles – their larval stage – live in water. Reptiles overcame this hurdle by developing tough shells for their eggs, encapsulating a watery environment for the growing embryo. Their eggs could be laid on dry land, miles from any water.

Later mammals took this a stage further. They carried their embryos inside them, giving them even greater flexibility and mobility.

Another important step for mammals was warm blood. Heat speeds up most chemical reactions, so the rate at which an organism can convert food into energy is dependent on its temperature. Cold-blooded animals like snakes and lizards rely largely on the sun for warmth, absorbing its heat directly into their bodies. When there is no sun to bask in, these creatures become very sluggish. Birds and mammals overcame this handicap by developing an internal central-heating system that kept the whole body at the optimum temperature for its metabolism. Being that much less dependent upon the physical environment, they could continue to be active in a wide variety of conditions and could inhabit regions too cold for reptiles.

The Freeing of Humanity

With human beings came new degrees of freedom. Language freed us from the need to learn only from our own experience. And our ability to deliberate upon the future gave us a certain freedom of will. We could choose those actions that offered us better chances of survival or enhanced our comfort and well-being.

Walking on two legs rather than four, we were creatures whose hands were free. We did not have to chase after our prey, we could set traps for it. We learnt to make our own fire, releasing us from a dependence on lightning strikes. Clothes allowed us to survive cooler climates. The wheel further enhanced our freedom of movement, and gave us the means to transport heavy loads with much less effort. Agriculture brought us other liberties, enabling us to raise our own animals, grow our own crops, and store the harvest for later use.

As we settled in communities we began to specialize our activities. Some caught the food, others prepared it. Some made the clothes, some collected water, others built new shelters. This increasing specialization brought greater efficiency, and with it yet greater emancipation from the constraints of the world. We could take on other activities such as pottery, smelting, forging, tanning, spinning, weaving, carving, healing, teaching, writing, painting, sculpture, and music-making.

More liberation came with the Industrial Revolution. No longer did we have to spend most of our time on the land; we could turn our energy and creativity to improving the quality of our lives. Machinery increased the efficiency of production, resulting in a plethora of material goods that allowed us to do many more tasks and achieve grander goals. New means of transport gave us yet greater mobility, and freed industry to use resources from around the globe. Medical discoveries relieved us of many diseases, freed us from much physical pain, and helped us recover from physical injury. We were steadily liberating ourselves from the constraints of our bodies and from many of the limits imposed by our environment.

Freedom from Toil

Today information technology is leading to emancipation from work itself. Automated factories produce cars, electric motors, television sets, radios, cameras, computers, and digital watches with almost no input of human energy. In banks, offices, warehouses, and supermarkets information technology is increasingly taking over functions previously performed by people. Accountants, lawyers, pilots, architects, draftsmen, doctors, engineers, and secretaries are being released from many of their routine tasks.

The consequence is plain to see. The more developed nations are no longer heading towards full employment but towards ever-increasing unemployment.

This does not, of course, spell the end of all work. What we cannot replace – and may never be able to replace – are the functions of the human heart and soul. Medicine may become more automated, but caring never can. Those services involving compassion, love, and understanding will continue to flourish – indeed they may for once be given the time they deserve. The creative arts in all their forms will still be the pursuit of humans rather than automata. And most crafts will continue, as a joy rather than a drudge. What will steadily decrease is the need to work in order to stay alive.

The Fear of Unemployment

Decreasing employment is often seen as a significant threat, both personally and socially – something to be fought against at all costs. But if you pause to think about it, this does not make sense.

From the dawn of civilization humanity has been striving to work less – not more. To this end we have invented a wealth of labor saving equipment – plows, windmills, waterwheels, pumps, weaving looms, milking machines, combine harvesters, lawnmowers, elevators, washing machines, food processors, microwave ovens, power drills, vacuum cleaners, electric can openers and pencil sharpeners, automatic car washes, and motorized golf carts to name just a few. The intention behind almost every technological development from the first stone axe to the automated bank teller has been to reduce the time and energy we spend in physical toil. Yet, now that we are finally seeing the fruits of our labor-saving, we are holding on fiercely to just what we have tried for so long to leave behind.

On the one hand we love work for what it brings – security, self-esteem, comforts, human contact, challenge. On the other hand we resent it for what it demands of us – the time we have to spend at it, the energy and freedom it seems to take from us. How many of us, if given the money we now receive from work, would still choose to spend our time in an office, a truck, a store, a print shop or a coal mine? The majority want what work gives, not the work itself.

We fear unemployment not because we fear the loss of work itself, but because we fear insecurity, uncertainty, loss of self-esteem, material discomfort and, on occasions, hunger – all things that work has helped us avoid. In addition, since our economies are based on the input of human labor (human time is the principal component of any price, the natural resources being intrinsically free), wide-scale unemployment can spell disaster for a nation's economic well-being.

The question we should be asking is not how to maintain employment, but how to create an economic system that can distribute resources and enhance our well-being without raping the planet – while at the same time fulfilling our age-old wish to be free from unwanted toil.

Freedom for What?

Freedom from toil is not the only freedom we have sought. We have fought to be free from oppression; fought to overthrow dictators and tyrants; fought for the freedom to vote for the government of our choice. Nations have battled to gain independence from other nations, erected statues to proclaim their liberty, and stamped it on their money. We have struggled for freedom from slavery, freedom from prejudice, and freedom from persecution. For the freedom to say what we believe, to live where we wish, and to worship as we choose.

But what is all this freedom for?

Our underlying motivation, as ever, is to move away from suffering towards greater happiness. This is the underlying freedom for which we have worked and fought. To be free from all that seems to stop us finding peace and fulfillment.

To an extent we have been successful. We have eliminated or reduced many sources of suffering. We have found ways to satisfy most of our body's needs. We have increased our standard of living. We have been able to fulfill many of our desires. But are we really happy? Even if we were all given a standard of living similar to that enjoyed by the average American, would we be truly happy and fulfilled?

The answer, of course, is 'No.' For reasons already discussed, our thinking is stuck in a materialist mindset, and it is to the service of this redundant belief that we turn our newfound liberties.

Take the case of our growing freedom from work. It is often suggested that this will allow us to spend more of our time in the pursuit of leisure. (Although it should not pass unnoticed that this is also perceived as leading to the growth of the 'leisure industry' and the opportunity to create more work!) For those indulging in leisure it certainly seems like the opposite to work. It is time to recover from our labors; a time to rest; a time of relief; a time for recreation. Working less will certainly be an opportunity to rest more, recover from centuries of exertion, and recreate our vitality. And humanity might well begin to sigh with relief. But what then? Have we really worked so hard and gained so much freedom only to spend the rest of our lives playing holographic video games or lying in the sun to our hearts' content?

No, our hearts would not be content for long. As long as we are caught in the trap of believing that inner peace comes through what we have or do, our minds will find things to concern themselves with. In this respect we are still far from free.

The Freedom to be Free

A mind that is caught up in the past is not free – no more free than a mind caught up in concerns about what might or might not happen in the future. A person worried about the opinions of others or anxious for security is not really free. We are not free if imagined fears drive our perception and our decisions. Nor is our thinking free if we judge someone on the basis of their race, dress, profession, accent, or hairstyle.

To be truly free we need to move beyond our conditioning – our culturally induced hypnosis, our outdated set of programs. We need to release ourselves from our attachment to time; our concern for past and future times. We need to be free of our dreams. Free from fear. Free to find what we most deeply seek. Free to be our true selves.

The freedom we now need is the freedom that allows us to think more intelligently, the inner freedom to express our creativity more fully and in more valuable ways. The freedom to follow our vision.

This is the freedom the world most needs. We saw at the

beginning of this second part of the book that humanity already has most of the understanding and technology necessary to avert environmental catastrophe. And we have the money. What we do not have is the will to do what we know is needed. And our will cannot be free if our minds are still attached to the material world.

Free will requires a free mind – not one trammeled by fear.

This is the opportunity that our physical freedoms are presenting us with – self-liberation. The freeing of our minds from the mental virus that causes us to misuse our creativity in so many insane ways.

However, before we become too euphoric, let us remember that whether or not we take this step is far from certain. Releasing the mind from its conditioning takes considerable inner work. In this respect we have not reached the end of work at all. There has merely been a shift in the field of work. Indeed, one might say that the real work – the work of awakening ourselves – is only just beginning.

RETURN TO NOW

Not I, not I, but the wind that blows through me!
A fine wind is blowing the new direction of Time.
If only I let it bear me, carry me, if only it carry me!
If only I am sensitive, subtle, Oh delicate, a winged gift!
If only, most lovely of all, I yield myself and am
    borrowed
By the fine, fine wind that takes its course through the
    chaos of the world
Like a fine, an exquisite chisel, a wedge-blade inserted;
If only I am keen and hard like the sheer tip of a wedge
Driven by invisible blows,
The rock will split, we shall come at the wonder, we
    shall find the Hesperides.
Oh, for the wonder that bubbles into my soul;
I would be a good fountain, a good well-head,
Would blur no whisper, spoil no expression.
What is the knocking?
What is the knocking at the door in the night?
It is somebody wants to do us harm.
No, no, it is the three strange angels.
Admit them, admit them.

D.H. Lawrence, The Song of a Man who has Come Through

AWAKENING – SELF-DEHYPNOSIS

The first problem for all of us, men and women, is not to learn, but to unlearn.

Gloria Steinem

In the preceding chapters we have considered how humanity's preoccupation with material progress and outer achievement can be seen as a form of cultural hypnosis. The values imparted to us through our upbringing, education, and social experience have seduced us into a set of assumptions about what is important, what we need, and what will bring us fulfillment. As a result we behave as if peace of mind comes from what we have and do, rather than from how we are.

Most of us can see the fallacy in this approach. We know that whether or not we remain calm and relaxed in a particular situation depends as much on how we perceive and interpret events as on the events themselves. But our conditioning is so pervasive that for much of the time our inner knowing remains hidden. We remain caught between what we have been taught and what we know.

The Hidden Observer

A parallel phenomenon occurs in ordinary hypnosis. In an experiment conducted by hypnosis researcher Dr. Ernest Hilgard, a subject was told that his left hand would feel no pain when placed in a bucket of ice-cold water. Anyone who has ever experienced ice-cold water will know that this can be very painful indeed, yet the subject reported that he felt fine; there was no pain. The hypnosis, it would seem, had been successful.

The subject was then asked to allow his right hand to engage in some 'automatic writing' – that is, without looking, to let the hand simply write anything that it wanted to. He started writing, 'It's freezing.' 'Ouch.' 'It hurts.' 'Take my hand out.' Although the hypnosis had elicited the desired behavior it had not, apparently, been able to override a deeper level of truth.

Hilgard called the unhypnotized part of the mind, the part that still felt the pain, the 'hidden observer.' His subjects described it as 'the part of me that looks at what is, and doesn't judge it,' and 'more like my real self, only more objective. When I'm in hypnosis, I'm imagining, letting myself pretend, but somewhere the hidden observer knows what's really going on.'

The same would seem to happen with our search for a more satisfying state of mind. The hidden observer within us knows that the key to fulfillment lies within. Yet this knowledge rarely comes to the surface and most of us continue to 'pretend' that outer well-being is the best path to inner fulfillment.

Until, that is, we engage in some automatic writing (or 'channeling' as some are wont to call it), when we may find ourselves expressing truths we did not know we knew. Or our hidden observer may reveal itself in other ways. It may speak to us in our dreams as images symbolic of our inner knowing. Deep in contemplation we may recognize the folly of our ways. Or liberated from our conditioned responses by a glass or two of wine or some other drug we may temporarily glimpse the inanity of the games we play.

It is as if a voice is there within us aching to be heard, but it cannot get past the clamor of our hypnotized thinking. The self-talk of the ego-mind is so busy describing what is happening, judging whether it is good or bad for us, and telling us what we should think and do, that there is little opportunity for our inner knowing to be heard. Instead we remain attached to our assumptions, dreaming of the fulfillment we believe they will bring.

Clinical versus Cultural Hypnosis

If we are to deal with the root cause of the crises now confronting us we must awaken from our trance and regain a more conscious contact with our own inner wisdom. We need the cultural equivalent of dehypnosis. But while waking from ordinary hypnosis is fairly straightforward – the hypnotist may count to three, click his fingers, and simply tell you to wake up – awakening from our cultural hypnosis is not nearly so simple.

For a start, there is no hypnotist waiting to awaken us. Much of our conditioning occurred long ago – some of it before we could speak or remember. And it has come through many different sources: parents, teachers, friends, strangers, books, magazines, radio, television, films, advertising. It is part of the fabric of our society. No single person was responsible.

Another very important difference between clinical and cultural hypnosis concerns the depth of the conditioning. In his book, *Waking Up*, the psychologist Charles Tart shows that ordinary hypnosis is a voluntary and limited relationship between consenting adults. The power given to the hypnotist is limited by time – usually to an hour or two – and by various ethical constraints – the subject does not expect to be bullied, threatened, or harmed. If the hypnosis does not work very well, the subject is not blamed. And, although a profound change in experience may occur for a short while, no basic or long-term changes in personality or 'reality' are expected by the subject – other than, perhaps, the relinquishing of some unwanted habit.

With our cultural hypnosis the situation is very different, as Tart elaborates. Our cultural consensus trance is not voluntary; it begins at birth without our conscious agreement. All authority is surrendered to the parents and other 'hypnotists,' who initially are regarded as omniscient and omnipotent. Induction is not limited to short sessions; it involves years of repeated reinforcement.

Clinical therapists would consider it highly unethical to use force, but our cultural hypnotists often do – a slap on the wrist or a good spanking for 'misbehaving.' Or they may use more subtle, but more powerful, emotional pressures – 'I will only love you if you think and behave as I tell you.'

Finally, and most significantly, the conditioning is intended to be permanent. It is meant to have a lasting effect on our personalities and the way we evaluate the world.

This is why awakening from our cultural trance entails far more than a simple snapping of the fingers. There is a lifetime's worth of extremely powerful induction to be transcended.

In some respects we would seem to be well and truly stuck. Indeed, for most of the time we are. Yet there are also times when Nature appears to snap her fingers for us. For a moment we wake up and see things in a different light. And have a taste of what lies ahead.

LETTING GO –
THE PARABLE OF THE ROPE

If being right is your goal,
   you will find error in the world,
   and seek to correct it.
But do not expect peace of mind.

If peace of mind is your goal,
   look for the errors in your beliefs and expectations.
   Seek to change them, not the world.
And be always prepared to be wrong.

A mind attached to its beliefs is like a person clinging to a piece of rope.

He holds on for dear life, knowing that if he were to let go he would fall to his death. His parents, his teachers, and many others have told him this is so; and when he looks around he can see everyone else doing the same.

Nothing would induce him to let go.

Along comes a wise person. She knows that holding on is unnecessary, that the security it offers is illusory, and only holds you where you are. So she looks for a way to dispel his illusions and help him to be free.

She talks of real security, of deeper joy, of true happiness, of peace of mind. She tells him that he can taste this if he will just release one finger from the rope.

'One finger,' thinks the man; 'that's not too much to risk for a taste of bliss.' So he agrees to take this first initiation.

And he does taste greater joy, happiness, and peace of mind.

But not enough to bring lasting fulfillment.

'Even greater joy, happiness and peace can be yours,' she tells him, 'if you will just release a second finger.'

'This,' he tells himself, 'is going to be more difficult. Can I do it? Will it be safe? Do I have the courage?' He hesitates, then, flexing his finger, feels how it would be to let go a little more . . . and takes the risk.

He is relieved to find he does not fall; instead he discovers greater happiness and inner peace.

But could more be possible?

'Trust me,' she says. 'Have I failed you so far? I know your fears, I know what your mind is telling you – that this is crazy, that it goes against everything you have ever learned – but please, trust me. Look at me, am I not free? I promise you will be safe, and you will know even greater happiness and contentment.'

'Do I really want happiness and inner peace so much,' he wonders, 'that I am prepared to risk all that I hold dear? In principle, yes; but can I be sure that I will be safe, that I will not fall?' With a little coaxing he begins to look at his fears, to consider their basis, and to explore what it is he really wants. Slowly he feels his fingers soften and relax. He knows he can do it. And he knows he must do it. It is only a matter of time until he releases his grip.

And as he does an even greater sense of peace flows through him.

He is now hanging by one finger. Reason tells him he should have fallen a finger or two ago, but he hasn't. 'Is there something wrong with holding on itself?' he asks himself. 'Have I been wrong all the time?'

'This one is up to you,' she says. 'I can help you no further. Just remember that all your fears are groundless.'

Trusting his quiet inner voice, he gradually releases the last finger.

And nothing happens.

He stays exactly where he is.

Then he realizes why. He has been standing on the ground all along.

And as he looks at the ground, knowing he need never hold on again, he finds true peace of mind.

PRESENCE –
A TIMELESS EXPERIENCE

'Are you a God?' they asked the Buddha. 'No,' he
replied.
'Are you an angel, then?' 'No.'
'A saint?' 'No.'
'Then what are you?'
Replied the Buddha, 'I am awake.'

Houston Smith

Many of us can remember times when we have been blessed with a
taste of self-liberation. The trigger might have been some spectacular scenery, a touching encounter, the birth of a child, or a
moment of tenderness. Whatever the reason – and sometimes there
is no apparent reason – we are taken out of ourselves and see things
without the layers of judgment and concern that usually cloud our
minds. In the words of the visionary poet William Blake, the doors
of perception are cleansed and we see things as they are – infinite.

In those special moments we feel more aware, in the present; no
longer lost in thoughts. There is a sense of release. Perhaps there are
feelings of awe and wonderment; a deeper connection with ourselves, with others, with Nature, and sometimes with the whole of
creation. We may remember what it is to be fully alive. In those
moments we are free. We are at ease.

Countless examples of such moments of grace are to be found in
autobiographies, poetry, and spiritual literature the world over.
Here is one from the historian Kenneth Clark:

It took place in the church of San Lorenzo, but did not seem to
be connected with the harmonious beauty of the architecture. I

can only say that for a few minutes my whole being was irradiated by a kind of heavenly joy, far more intense than anything I had known before. . . . that I had 'felt the finger of God' I am quite sure, and, although the memory of this experience has faded, it still helps me to understand the joys of the saints.

Margaret Isherwood recalled an experience she had when she was nine years old:

Suddenly the Thing happened, and as everybody knows, it cannot be described in words. The Bible phrase, 'I saw the heavens open' seems as good as any if not taken literally. I remember saying to myself, in awe and rapture, 'so it's like this; now I know what heaven is like, now I know what they mean in church.'

The Indian poet Rabindranath Tagore was watching the sun rise in a Calcutta street when,

suddenly, in a moment, a veil seemed to be lifted from my eyes. . . . The thick cloud of sorrow that lay on my heart in many folds was pierced through and through by the light of the world.... There was nothing and no one whom I did not love at that moment.

And Warner Allen, in his book, *The Timeless Moment*, describes a flash of illumination that occurred during a performance of Beethoven's Seventh Symphony. Again he found his experience hard to describe:

A dim impression of the condition of the objective self might be given by a jumble of incoherent sentences. 'Something has happened to me – I am utterly amazed – can this be that? (*That* being the answer to the riddle of life) – but it is too simple – I always knew it – it is remembering an old forgotten secret – like coming home – I am not "I," not the "I" I thought – there is no death – peace passeth all understanding.'

Common to the majority of such experiences is the fact that they came unbidden. I did nothing to make it happen. It came upon me completely effortlessly. In such moments waking up seems so easy.

Two Sides of a Fence

The reality of our day-to-day waking consciousness and these moments of liberation are so different it is almost as if a mental fence divides the two. On one side of the fence I am caught in my mind; in my thoughts, my anxieties, my judgments, and my fears. I may on occasion recognize that this is unnecessary and that it takes me away from the present moment; but such understanding is seldom sufficient to release my mind from the grip of conditioning. So deeply ingrained is my attachment to what I believe I should be thinking and doing there seems no way over that fence. Indeed, for much of the time I have totally forgotten there is another way of being.

But when, for one reason or another, I find myself on the other side of the fence, it all seems so simple. It is clear that I need do nothing to feel at ease and at peace. I know I am at peace. And I know that nothing can threaten this peace, for it is a quality of life itself, not something that can be created or destroyed. All I need do is to relax and let go of my fears. How, I wonder, could I ever have got myself so caught up?

In this state of consciousness the true meaning of non-attachment is apparent. It is not, as it is often interpreted, a withdrawal from one's surroundings – a lack of concern, a lack of responsibility, or a lack of feeling. It is simply that I am no longer attached to the idea that what goes on around me determines whether or not I am content. In this state I am free to respond to the needs of others without the aura of self-concern that dogs so much of our thinking. Mahatma Gandhi put it very clearly:

Detachment is not apathy or indifference. It is the prerequisite for effective involvement. Often what we think is best for others is distorted by our attachment to our opinions: we want others to be happy in the way we think they should be happy. It is only when we want nothing for ourselves that we are able to see clearly into others' needs and understand how to serve them.

Timeless Wisdom

Gandhi's ideas were not new. His philosophy was drawn from the *Bhagavad Gita*, one of India's ancient spiritual texts. The reason we are confused and suffer, says the *Gita*, is because we are caught in the conflicts that arise from attachment to the fruits of our actions. To develop both wisdom and compassion we need to awaken to our true Self. Then we can act according to the demands of the situation at hand, rather than the demands of an ever-vulnerable ego.

In one way or another this is what all the great religions have been trying to tell us. They may couch it in different terms, clothe it in different doctrines, teach it through different metaphors, and approach it through different practices, but they share the same underlying goal. It is to leave behind self-centered desires and be free from our attachment to material things. It is to rise above suffering. To open to a higher wisdom and reconnect with the essence of Life. It is to regain our vitality.

The essence of these teachings is not determined by time or culture – although these may influence its form and expression. It is determined by the essential nature of the mind. And this is the same now as it was five thousand years ago.

One of the intrinsic qualities of consciousness is, according to Indian teachings, *ananda*, usually translated as 'bliss,' the perfect happiness. It is the peace that passeth all understanding – not so much because it cannot be understood, although this may be true, but because it lies beyond all thinking and all understanding. And, like matter continually gravitating towards itself, mind is continually attracted towards a state of greater happiness – that is towards itself.

At first people are not aware of what it is they are really after. Because they are only dimly awake to the realities within, they think that fulfillment lies in their interaction with the world. This inevitably leads to an attachment to whatever it is they imagine will bring the happiness they know they want.

Many remain caught up in such dreams for the whole of their lives. But there are always a few who, through good fortune or otherwise, pass through this phase and awaken to a fuller appreciation of themselves – and ultimately to the real nature of Mind. Not wanting to see others remain caught in suffering, these wise ones have tried to help others attain a similar liberation, recounting their own experiences and proffering advice on how to let go of attachment and fear. And there have been a few whose expressions of this eternal wisdom so caught people's hearts and souls that their teachings resonated across the world and down through history.

Back to the Present

There is another sense in which this wisdom is 'timeless.' It is the undoing of our 'timefulness.' It offers release from our bondage to past and future – a return to the present moment.

The thirteenth-century Christian mystic Meister Eckhart described how in moments of inner quiet

> There exists only the present instant . . . a Now which always and without end is itself new . . . There is no yesterday nor any tomorrow, but only Now, as it was a thousand years ago and as it will be a thousand years hence.

And six hundred years later Richard Jefferies wrote:

> It is eternity now, I am in the midst of it. It is about me in the sunshine; I am in it, as the butterfly in the light-laden air. Nothing has to come; it is now. Now is eternity; now is immortal life.

In some senses, of course, we are always in the present. Our past we know from memories, but those memories are experienced in the present, just as our future is something we imagine in the present. Whatever we may be thinking and doing we are doing it 'now.' Even when we are totally wrapped up in thoughts about past or future, the thoughts themselves are happening 'now.'

When we say we are not in the present we really mean that our attention is not in the 'now.' It is looking back to the past or forward to the future. To return to the present is to return our attention to the here and now.

The mind that is attending to the present is a mind that is free from distracting self-talk about what has or has not happened or what might or might not happen.

And it is not just our internal dialogue about past or future that holds our attention away from the present. Self-talk about the present can be equally distracting.

Two Zen monks were paying a visit to some ancient hot springs. It was a clear night, the moon was full, the water was a perfect temperature. Gazing up at the sky one monk marvelled at the fact that for centuries people had visited this spot and enjoyed its beauty – many on full-moon nights just like this. The joy the two were now experiencing was not theirs alone, it was a joy shared across time. And so he sat, meditating on the timeless quality of their joy.

After a while the second monk responded: 'Even better to enjoy it.'

The Peace of Now

A mind in the present moment is free to experience 'what is.' This does not imply that one no longer takes any notice of the past, nor considers the future. There is still much to learn from the past, and there are still many ways we can influence the future and so improve the quality of our lives and the lives of others. The difference is that, once liberated from its state of trance, the mind no longer finds itself lost in fruitless concerns for these other times.

In the present we stop holding on to all those ropes we think will save us. Instead we recognize that all along we have been standing on the ground – the ground of our own being. There is no longer any need to derive our identity from our interactions with the world. How others see us does not alter our existence. This level of being needs no qualification or recognition. Nor can it be threatened. It will always be there whatever may happen.

Knowing our inner essence to be invulnerable, the mind is not caught up in concern. And a mind free from concern is a mind at peace.

In the present we find what we have been seeking all along.

Enlightened

Being able to experience reality as it is, undistorted by our hopes and fears, is often referred to as 'enlightenment.' The word 'light' in this term is usually thought of in the sense of illumination. A mind that is enlightened is said to be an 'illumined' mind. It is a mind that has 'seen the light,' or sees things in a new light.

There is, however, another sense of the word 'enlighten' that is equally appropriate. That is 'a lightening of the load.'

The heaviest burdens in this life are not our physical burdens but our mental ones. We are weighed down by our concern for the past, and our worries about the future. This is the load we bear, the weariness that comes from our timefulness.

To enlighten the mind is to relieve it of this load. An enlightened mind is a mind no longer weighed down by attachments; it is a mind that is free.

Being free, it is a mind that is no longer so serious about things – it takes things more lightly.

Could this be why enlightened people laugh and smile more than the rest of us do?

A Shift in Perception

From either perspective – that of illumination or that of lightening the load – the essence of enlightenment is a shift in perception. It is a shift from seeing the world through the eyes of concern, with all their embellishment, suppression, and interpretation, to seeing without judgment; seeing what is rather than what ought to be or might be.

A permanent shift of perception is, however, a very different thing from the taste of it we are offered in our moments of grace. Our conditioning is deep and no single sunset or close personal encounter is going to undo it. As almost everyone who has been blessed with such moments of illumination has discovered, it is not long before our ordinary mode of consciousness returns.

Later perhaps, some other event may suddenly trigger the mind to let go of its attachments and fears. But there is no telling when that might occur – we might have to wait a very long time.

But we do not have time to wait for rainbows. Nor, unlike the inhabitants of Aldous Huxley's *Island,* do we have mynah birds flying around repeatedly reminding us 'Here and now, boys!' 'Attention!' If we are to step beyond our collective trance – as we must if we are to have any hope of resolving the crisis this mode of thinking has brought upon us – it is imperative that we seek to make a more enlightened consciousness our daily consciousness.

This, as we shall see later, may be the true purpose of time. Not spending it looking for peace through what we have or do, but seeking liberation from our belief that what we have or do will bring us peace.

In principle, we can make this shift of perception at any time we choose. Whenever we are caught up in trying to make the future the way we want it to be – which, in one way or another, is most of the time – we have the opportunity to look at things differently. Rather than wondering, 'How can I get such-and-such so that I can be happy?' we could ask, 'Even if I were to get what I want, would I then be at peace?' And, 'If I do not get what I want, can I still be at peace?'

If there is a willingness to look at things differently the answers to these questions are nearly always 'No' and 'Yes.' Then, having let go of our anxiety about the future, our attention is once again free to return to the here and now.

That much is easy. The difficulty comes in remembering to stop and ask. This is where we need the practice. And for most of us the area of life that offers us the most opportunity for practice – and where we most need help – is in our personal relationships. For it is here that we come up against some of our deepest conditioning and some of our strongest judgments.

LOVE –
LETTING GO OF JUDGMENT

Love is not something you do,
It is not how you behave.
There's nothing you can do that constitutes loving
    another,
No action that is of itself loving.
Love is a way of being.
And more than that.
It is simply being,
Being with another person, however they may be.
Holding no judgments, having no agendas,
No need to have them experience your love,
No desire to demonstrate love,
No intrusion upon their soul.
Nothing but a total acceptance of their being,
Born of your acceptance of yours.

When we say that people make judgments about others we can
mean two things. There are the evaluations we make of a person's
behavior, appearance, and other personal attributes. This is the kind
of assessment we make when, for instance, we weigh up the
advantages and disadvantages of employing a particular person for
a job. Do they have the necessary skills and experience? How will
they respond under pressure? Are they trustworthy? Will they fit in
to the culture? Such appraisals can be most valuable – without them
we might make many errors.

    The second type is made according to criteria set by our own
inner needs. It is the assessment we make as to whether someone
might help or hinder us in our search for personal fulfillment. Thus
I might judge an inflexible bureaucrat who causes me considerable

inconvenience and stands in the way of my getting what I want as 'stupid' or 'uncaring.' Conversely, one who goes out of his way to be of assistance I might judge as 'kind' and 'friendly.'

The problem with such judgments is that we all too easily project them onto the other person. We take our reaction to their words and deeds and on that basis make a judgment of them as a human being. In general terms, if we like the person and think they are 'on our side' we categorize them as a 'good' person. Conversely, if we dislike them or think they stand in the way of our fulfillment, we are liable to put them in the category of 'bad' – someone who needs improvement.

Such judgments of another's being are never valid. They are a projection of our own mind; our own hopes and fears. Someone else, with different hopes and different fears, might see the same person in another light. How many times have we been surprised to find someone disliking a person we think highly of; or conversely, liking a person we have judged as a waste of time?

Since they are of our own making, such judgments may bear no relation to the truth. For all I know, the inflexible bureaucrat may have been preoccupied with a domestic crisis and later have regretted the way he treated me. Conversely, the more amenable person may have been trying to manipulate me for his own ends.

To judge another person's worth as a human being is never justified. We may like or dislike another's appearance, personality, and beliefs but this has no bearing on their value as a being. And we have no right to make such judgments. No being has any greater or lesser value than any other being.

Not only are such judgments not justified, they are not that helpful. They keep us from seeing the other person in the present moment. Instead we see them through the eyes of the past and our concerns for the future. We do not see them as they really are.

An Experiment

Think of a friend. Anyone will do; either sex, any age. The first person who comes into your mind will serve perfectly well.

Pause for a moment and consider the thoughts you have about them. Consider their looks. . . . The way they dress. . . . Their habits. . . . The way they speak. . . . And anything else that comes to mind about them.

Notice the feelings you have towards them.

Consider the various things that you like about this person. What makes them a friend?

Notice those things that you do not appreciate so much. The changes that would improve them in your eyes.

Then pause to remember that all these thoughts are based on past experience. You are projecting the past on to that person. As a result you are not actually appreciating them as they are.

Now – and this may take a little more time – take one of these judgments, recognize that it has been derived from past impressions, and ask: Is that how this person really is? Is that how they experience themselves? Or is it simply the picture I have made of them – the picture I have projected onto them?

Ask this about the various other judgments that you make of that person, trying each time to step beyond your interpretations and really see them as they are.

To get value from this exercise it's worth taking a few minutes right now to sit quietly and explore these questions.

You may discover that the more you let go of your judgments of the other person and perceive them with a more open mind, the more you begin to understand them. And the more you understand them and accept them as they are, the closer you feel towards them. This is not to say that you may not already have felt close, but there may now be a deeper sense of closeness – a feeling of empathy and compassion towards the other. You are beginning to perceive them with a more open heart.

It can also be a great help to repeat the exercise focussing on someone that you do not know so well. As you let go of preconceptions about who and how they might be, a new sense of empathy and openness can emerge. You begin to understand what it really means to love a stranger – or even to love an enemy. It is not a romantic love or a love full of infatuation; it is a love based on the simple acceptance of another being as they are.

Love and Judgment

We have already seen two ways in which our concern for whether or not the world will give us what we want can disturb us. It keeps us from being at peace; and it takes our attention away from the present moment. We are now seeing a third way in which it can get in our own way. The judgments it leads us to make stand in the way of love.

Love, whether it be the love of a child for its mother, of two lovers for each other, or a love for Nature, is born of a sense of oneness. It is an expression of a deeper sense of connection. And its goal is unity – to be one with that which one loves.

When we judge another person we see the ways in which their thoughts, words, and deeds – and by implication their feelings, desires, and goals – differ from our own. In our minds we see separation rather than oneness. Such separation does not engender love.

The opposite to love is not hate but judgment. Hate is just a common consequence of judgment.

Unconditional Love

Much of what we call love is highly conditional. It is conditional upon the way a person behaves, the way they look, the values they profess, and perhaps the feelings they have for us. We love them for their appearance, their manner, their mind, their body, their talents, their smell, their dress, and, should they agree with our own, their beliefs and values. The more they match our expectations of the perfect person, the more we love them.

Such love turns the other person into someone special – someone who in our eyes shines out above the others. Yet all this specialness is just a form of judgment. We have judged them as fascinating, sensitive, wise, kind, honest, good-looking, fashionable, sexy, humorous, selfless, artistic, intelligent, understanding, or whatever else appeals to our ego-mind. We have judged them as someone who will satisfy our needs.

Unconditional love, on the other hand, does not depend upon how a person thinks, feels, or behaves. It does not pause to assess whether or not another is worthy of affection.

It recognizes that beneath all our various appearances and activities we each seek the same thing – a more satisfying state of mind. Here we are all the same – and all equally loveable.

Unconditional love also acknowledges that we are all, to some extent or other, caught in the trap of believing that our inner satisfaction is determined by what goes on around us. Each of us may feel the need for security, control, recognition, approval, and stimulus to varying degrees, and may feel threatened by things that seem to stand in the way of our fulfillment. It recognizes that we each make mistakes from time to time, and that we each experience suffering in some form or other.

In this respect we know each other as well as we know ourselves. This is the source of true compassion.

The Love of God

This love is the love of which the great religions have spoken – the love of God. If God (and we each have our own interpretations of that word) exists and loves us, It does not love us because of something we have done. It does not judge us as good or bad. Such judgments stem from our own needs, not God's.

Nor does It love us depending upon how much attention we give It. That is merely another projection of our needs. The love of God is the love of our being, of the inner essence that permeates us all. It is love for the dreamer – not for the dream.

This is the love we each seek. And it is the way in which we want others to love us. We want to be loved as we are, warts and all; not for something we have said or done, or might say or do.

Moreover, it is the way we would like to love. To have the love of God is to have unconditional love in our own hearts. We want to be able to love in this way because inside we know that it is lasting and more deeply satisfying than any conditional love.

But how do we attain such love? That is the eternal challenge. How do we learn to love our neighbor as we love as ourselves?

One path, available to most of us but not usually given the recognition it is due, is our personal relationships.

RELATIONSHIPS –
THE YOGA OF THE WEST

Those wise ones who see that the consciousness within
themselves is the same consciousness within all
conscious beings, attain eternal peace.

Katha Upanishad

Richard Alpert (otherwise known as Ram Dass) once remarked
that 'Relationships are the yoga of the West.' The Sanskrit word
yoga means 'union' and in Indian philosophy 'a yoga' is a path that
leads to union – union with Brahman, the essence of creation and
the essence of one's own self.

The reason why personal relationships offer such a path to
Westerners is twofold. First, they are one of the most important
issues in our lives. We long in our hearts for deep connection with
others. And when that connection is alive it can be the greatest joy
in life, something we value above all else. Yet many also find that
personal relationships bring our greatest anxieties; and when they
deteriorate or fail, our greatest sorrow and pain.

Second, it is in our more intimate relationships that some of the
less-welcome repercussions of our misguided thinking come to the
surface. It is an area where growth is sorely needed. And not just for
our own benefit. If we still have problems relating to the person we
profess to love, what hope is there that we can relate properly to
those of other cultures, and to all the other living beings with
whom we share this planet?

Trance Relationships

Most of us have at one time or another experienced some of the rather 'unloving' behavior to which our relationships can lead. Deceiving each other in order not to have our security threatened; hiding our thoughts and feelings as well as our past actions. Trying to prove we are better in some way. Fighting to prove some belief or point of view. Manipulating the other so that they will behave as we want and give us what we think we need. Not being ourselves, but how our partner would like us to be. Saying things we do not believe in order to win approval.

Such patterns stem from the conditional nature of our love. In much the same way as we create fear and stress for ourselves whenever we perceive our needs to be threatened, we may create feelings of love for someone who appears to meet our needs. Then, in order that the one we 'love' stays around and delivers our fulfillment, we play the same game in reverse. We try to match their needs and expectations. We do and say the right things and try to be the right sort of person – clever, witty, sincere, strong, caring, or whatever else we think they want. We want to be their special person. The one they want to be with.

Such love is very fragile. Should our partner not do as we would wish or otherwise fail to meet some dream we have of them, we can easily find ourselves slipping into the opposite reaction. Fear raises its head once again and we find ourselves becoming upset with them and falling out of love.

If we are not very careful – and most of us are not – our partner's failure to fulfill the function we have set is interpreted as an unjustified attack, and a too hasty response on our part can lead us into unnecessary and frequently disruptive behavior. We may try to defend ourselves – perhaps by returning an attack or criticizing them in some way. We may withdraw our affection, withholding from them what they need. Or we try to make them feel guilty, in the hope that they will change and once more satisfy our needs. We may even wonder what we saw in them in the first place.

But if they are as inwardly vulnerable as we are (which is probable), they may well perceive our reaction as an equally unjustified attack on them. And, if not careful, they are likely to find themselves responding in similar ways. All too easily we become caught in a vicious circle of resentment and blame.

Little wonder that many such relationships break down.

Such behaviors are not limited to our romantic relationships. Similar patterns occur in many of our other relationships – with our family, our friends, our colleagues at work. Here again we can find ourselves reacting out of need and fear – and with similar disruptive consequences.

But damaging as they may be, we can also turn these reactions to good effect. Our disagreeable responses and strange behaviors can – if we care to look – reveal our inner vulnerabilities. They can help us become aware of our hidden fears; and through exploring our fears we can begin to see the various psychological attachments we have formed. Thus each strange reaction can be an opportunity to grow and mature.

Seen in this light our personal relationships can become our *yoga* – a path from attachment toward self-liberation.

Spiritual Relationships

Turning a close relationship into a path of self-liberation necessi- tates a change in our perception of our partner. Instead of seeing him or her as someone who might satisfy our various imagined needs, we can begin to see them as someone who can help us fulfill our real quest – our quest for fulfillment. They are offering us the opportunity to notice our attachments and the ways in which they distort our perception and our thinking.

Such opportunities do not come when our relationships are running smoothly; they come in those moments when we are unhappy or upset with our partner. At such moments we may well see the other as an enemy rather than a friend. But they are only an enemy of the ego-mind. As such they are more of a true friend than we might at first suppose. Not the friend who can fulfill our illusory needs, but the friend who can help us awaken from our dreams.

This brings us to a second way in which those we are close to can be of help. They know better than anyone our attachments, our dreams, and our fears. Through their understanding and compas- sion – remember, they have *their* attachments and vulnerabilities – our partners can help us see when we are stuck, and help us step back and look at what is going on inside. As our spiritual allies they can help us see our negative reactions to be the consequences of our dreams. And, given trust, they can help us recognize our errors and awaken to our inner truth.

Forgiveness

A third way in which our partners can be of help is in presenting us with a continuing exercise in letting go. Whenever we find ourselves thinking that they have said or done wrong, we can try to step back for a moment and appreciate that they are, in their own way, seeking the same as we are seeking. The only difference is in the way they go about it – and the kind of mistakes they make.

This is the essence of forgiveness. It is not saying 'I know you committed a sin, but I will not hold it against you.' It is recognizing that there was no sin, merely a mistake – and we all make mistakes in our search for peace. Forgiveness is acknowledging that I too, given the same history and circumstances, could easily have made a similar mistake.

The same sentiment is expressed in the New Testament. The Greek word that we translate as 'forgiveness,' *aphesis*, means 'to let go.' And the word for 'sin' is *amartano*. This, as Maurice Nichol pointed out in his book, *The Mark*, is a term derived from archery meaning to have missed the mark, to have missed the target. The target we are each seeking is inner fulfillment, but, imagining this will come from what we have or do, we aim in the wrong direction, and so 'miss the mark.' It is this fundamental error as to how to find happiness and peace of mind that is our 'original sin.'

To forgive others their sins is to recognize they have merely missed the mark. It is to let go of the judgment that they have wronged us; and to recognize instead that they are as caught up in illusions as we are.

Forgiveness is also a letting go of our belief that another person has upset us – as if they had such power. It is to take responsibility for our own distress, recognize it for what it is, and so change our perception.

Practicing Forgiveness

Forgiveness is not an easy practice. As anyone who has trodden this path knows, it requires commitment, vigilance, and patience.

It also requires continual self-reminding. Once someone or something has triggered one of our inner vulnerabilities it is all too easy to forget our higher goal. We forget our practice – only to remember later how we could have seen things differently.

On those occasions when we do remember that our interpre-tation of events determines our reaction, we can help ourselves by pausing to ask our 'hidden observer' whether it can suggest another way of seeing the other person. As ever, you have to watch out for the ego-mind and its distortions, but if you listen carefully you can sometimes hear the small, quiet voice of the unhypnotized self. And what it usually says – though often not in words – is that here is another being, like you, seeking love. Suddenly you see them in an altogether different light. They seem totally changed. Yet they have done nothing; it is only you who have changed.

This is not to imply that changing our perception will resolve all the difficulties we encounter in our relationships. Letting go of our judgments may make another person's errors understandable, but it does not make them right. However, if we can approach such issues from a genuine love rather than from anger and resentment, the chances of our being able to help them in their own growth are likely to be much greater.

Sometimes we may find that our partner continues to seek satisfaction in ways that we cannot live with. Nevertheless, when we do decide to go our own way we still have a choice as to how we separate. We can separate with bad feelings, blaming the other's faults and unacceptable behavior. Or we can separate with forgive-ness, love, and understanding.

Forgiveness in such circumstances can be quite difficult. The ego's mode of thinking has usually taken a very firm hold of our minds – it is probably telling us that our anger is quite justified. Often there is not even room to consider the possibility of seeing the other person in a different light, let alone making that shift. But if you can find unconditional love in such difficult times as these you will find yourself taking a big step towards your own inner liberation.

All Our Relations

Such practice is not limited to our intimate personal relationships. The same principles apply to our relationships with people we hardly know, or may have never even met.

To take just one example, I have never met the political leader of my country. However, I have read much about him in the press, seen him on television, and heard some of the things he has said. As a result I have formed a good many impressions of him. And I have opinions as to ways in which he is right, and ways in which he is wrong. But all of this is my projection. I do not know what goes on inside his mind, how he sees the world, what he knows that I do not know. I do not know what his personal hopes and fears are, or why he makes the decisions he does. I can only surmise that, given his own history, experiences, and conditioning, he is doing the best he knows how.

This does not mean that I agree with his actions. If I feel that certain policies do not serve people as well as others might, I will do whatever seems most appropriate to try to change the situation. On the other hand, I also try not to let my judgment of his decisions become a judgment of him as a person. I try – and frequently it is not easy – to see him as another fellow being seeking peace.

We can practice the same with complete strangers – people we see in the street, on a bus or plane, in a restaurant. We can practise seeing past their actions and appearances, past the judgments we project on to them, and see that invisible part of them that is in so many ways just like ourselves. The results can be most surprising.

Similarly with non-human beings. The dogs, dolphins, and dragonflies we meet are also conscious beings. They may not have developed the same mode of consciousness as we have. They have different senses which give them different experiences of reality; and they have different ways of interacting with the world, giving a different color to their consciousness. Nevertheless the essence of consciousness remains the same; it is the essence of being aware, the light behind all experience.

Self-Love

Finally let us not forget that we are in a continuous relationship with ourselves. As many have commented, we cannot love the world if we do not first love ourselves. But how do we love ourselves? Is it conditional or unconditional love?

You may gain some insight by repeating the exercise on page 129 in relation to yourself. What criticisms do I have of myself? What do I approve of about myself? How do these judgments, coming as they do from my own past, prevent me from appreciating myself in the present moment?

Certainly there have been many times when we have made

mistakes – many times when we have 'missed the mark' and not found the happiness we seek. But we need not berate ourselves for them. If we can cease judging ourselves and understand how it was we came to react as we did, we can begin to forgive ourselves.

And then, as we begin to understand ourselves a little better, we may find ourselves drawn to another question: What is this self that we love?

And who is the self that is doing the loving?

MEDITATION –
THE ART OF NOTHING

In order that the mind should see light instead of
darkness, so the entire soul must be turned away from
this changing world, until its eye can learn to
contemplate reality and that supreme splendor which
we have called the good. Hence there may well be an
art whose aim would be to effect this very thing.

Socrates

In addition to our character, our personality, our habits, our beliefs, the mistakes we have made, the hopes we have, and all the other things that go towards our sense of being an individual self, there is a dimension to our identity that we cannot describe so easily. This is the 'I' that is the experiencer, the one prerequisite of any experience. To become more directly acquainted with this transcendental self – and thus approach the underlying truth of our existence – is a common aim of various techniques of meditation. Their goal is to bring mental activity to an end and so reach what Indian teachings describe as *samadhi* – a state of 'still mind.'

A still mind is a mind that is free from fear, free from fantasies, free from ruminations over the past, free from concern about what may or may not be happening to it. It is a mind no longer disturbed by the many thoughts that come from believing that fulfillment lies in what we have or what we do. For once, the ego-mind has fallen silent.

Consciousness itself remains. You are still awake; still aware. You, the experiencer, still exist. You simply are no longer lost in your thoughts. You are free to know yourself as you are. Here is your true identity. The Self is known for what it is; the self-existent one, the essence of consciousness.

Such knowing comes not as an idea or an understanding, for that would make the subject of experience an object of experience. Besides, the still mind is a mind that is not moved by ideas or understandings – at least, not as we normally think of them. This knowing comes from a direct acquaintance. One simply is. One is not any thing; there is no substance or form to one's being. But its reality is absolutely clear – and undeniable.

It is this transcendence of the ego and remembering of one's underlying nature that gives meditation its value. Here is the security, identity, and peace we have been looking for all along. Here is the fulfillment for which we have been yearning. And with this taste of inner truth we return to the world a little less attached to it.

No single moment of transcendence is likely to enlighten us forever. Our conditioning is so deep and the attraction of the world so strong that it does not take long before we once again are caught up in the machinations of the ego-mind, and once again start looking for external sources of fulfillment. But a little of the taste remains, and our attachments to the world may not be quite as strong as they were before. And perhaps after another taste, a little less strong still. This is why regular meditation practice is usually recommended – a daily dose of dehypnosis – a daily remembering of ourselves in our unconditioned state.

Different not Difficult

Meditation is often thought of as an *activity* of the mind, some form of mental 'doing.' However, a mental activity does not easily lead to a state of stillness; and meditative practices which take this approach tend to be very difficult. True meditation is not difficult so much as different – completely different from the mental processes we are accustomed to.

Most techniques aimed at stilling the mind are exercises in attention rather than exercises in thinking. One does not quieten the mind by changing what one thinks, but by changing the direction and quality of one's attention. In their own particular ways meditation techniques shift the attention away from the world of the senses – the world that we think will bring us peace of mind – and turn it in towards itself.

As the mind begins to settle down it discovers an inner calm and peace. The attention has found what it has been seeking along, and needs no coercion to continue in this direction. This is reflected in the following lines by Maharishi Mahesh Yogi, the teacher of Transcendental Meditation, taken from his book *The Science of Being and Art of Living*.

To go to a field of greater happiness is the natural tendency of the mind. Because in the practice of transcendental meditation the conscious mind is set on the way to experiencing bliss-consciousness, the mind finds the way increasingly attractive as it advances in the direction of bliss. It finds increasing charm at every step of its march. This practice is, therefore, not only simple but also automatic.

Practice

In this respect the art of meditation can be the essence of easiness. It is just letting go – allowing the mind to return to its natural state of its own accord.

Any difficulty that may be experienced usually comes from the difficulty involved in unhooking the attention from its conditioned thinking. So strong is our attachment to finding happiness through our sensory experience – and this includes not just what we experience through our eyes, ears, and skin, but also the things we see, hear, and feel in our imagination – that the mind holds on hard to its cherished thoughts.

Even when we do let go and the mind begins to relax and settle down, it usually is not long before it is disturbed again as some unfulfilled desire starts once more to work out ways of finding future satisfaction. In this respect stilling the mind is not at all easy.

This is why specific techniques of meditation are of value – not as things to do, but as aids to release the mind from its deeply ingrained patterns. They are skills we can learn to disengage our egoic mode of thinking.

Normally we are so full of time – so full of all our 'doing' – we seldom pause to take the time to reconnect with ourselves. But when we do, we discover that since the still mind is changeless, and since it is only through change that we know time, this state of *samadhi* is one in which time has ceased to exist. There is only the present moment, a state without duration. A state of true time-lessness.

This timelessness is more than just a state of mind. We shall see shortly that, much as it may contradict our daily experience, we are in essence timeless beings. Not only are we not *what* we think we are, we are also not *where* or *when* we think we are.

I –
NOWHERE AND NOWHEN

The body is always in time, the spirit is always timeless
and the psyche is an amphibious creature compelled by
the laws of man's being to associate itself to some
extent with its body, but capable, if it so desires, of
experiencing and being identified with its spirit and,
through its spirit, with the divine Ground.

Aldous Huxley

What does it mean to be an experiencing entity? Is each of us simply
an isolated consciousness, bound by space and time to the body we
inhabit? One among five billion other self-conscious individuals
who have been given a brief window of experience onto this world
– a brief opportunity to satisfy our desires?

If that is all we are, no wonder we fear death. No wonder we fear
anything that seems to prevent us finding peace. No wonder we
become so upset with anyone who stands in the way of our having
what we want. No wonder we cling to our attachments. No wonder
we seek to control the world around us in order to find fulfillment.
No wonder we try to squeeze as much juice as possible out of
everything we do. For what else is there?

If this is the truth of our existence, no wonder we take drugs –
drugs to relieve us of our depression and help us forget that this is
all we are, drugs to enhance our experience of our meagre few
decades. No wonder some of us have no qualms about mistreating,
abusing, and even killing other human beings. No wonder some
people commit suicide.

But is this all we are?

Can we be sure that our individual self is not part of some eternal universal consciousness temporarily peeking out through the senses of this body into the physical world around?

Can we be sure that the same consciousness is not simultaneously peeking out through each of the other five billion human nervous systems on this planet, through the hundred billion human beings that have gone before us, and through all the other sentient creatures on this planet and across the Universe?

Could my sense of separateness be just an illusion? I may believe I am here in my body, located at this particular point in space and time. But can I be so sure?

Where Are You Now?

Ask yourself this: 'Where am I?'

You might well reply, 'Right here, of course. The particular spot where I am now.'

But is that where you are? It may be where your body is; but where exactly are 'you'? Where is your inner self – the inner observer of all your experiences?

'Somewhere in my head' is a common answer. This is where most people experience themselves to be. It also accords with our knowledge that what we experience is closely related to what takes place in our brains. But to conclude that the self is where the brain is would be an error.

Consider the following thought-experiment.* Suppose that your eyes were transplanted to your belly, your ears to your hips, and your nose to your navel. Imagine yourself observing the world through these senses. Where would you now experience yourself to be? In your head? Or in your belly?

Somewhere in the belly area seems the obvious answer.

Consider a second thought-experiment. Imagine your optic nerves connected to a television camera, your auditory nerves to microphones, your olfactory nerves to chemical sensors, and your

---

* 'Thought-experiments' are experiments conducted within one's own imagination. As such they can often give valuable insights into situations where physical experiments would be very difficult or impossible.

Albert Einstein often made use of thought-experiments, and through them came to some of his most important insights. Imagining himself in a continually accelerating elevator led to the realization that gravity and acceleration were indistinguishable. This was the seed for his 'General Theory of Relativity.'

tactile nerves to pressure and temperature sensitive membranes, so that all your sensory data now came from this set of artificial senses.

Then imagine this equipment being fitted to a robot. And imagine this robot being located in the room next door. Where would you now *experience* yourself to be?

In the room next door, presumably. That is the origin of all my sensory data – the source of the information I have concerning location.

Where, then, are 'you,' the self that is experiencing the room next door? Are you still in the original room where your body and brain are? Or are you in the room next door?

If you reply that you would be wherever your body and brain are, you must then ask how you know where they are? The only data you now have about the original room is from memory. You have no present experience of that room. For all you know I might have moved your body into another room. You would have no knowledge whatsoever of this other room, and would have no thought of being there. In this case your thought that you were still in the first room would be wrong.

The other answer seems more correct. You would be where you experience yourself to be: in the other room where your 'senses' are. You would experience yourself as being somewhere behind the television camera, between the microphones, inside the membrane on the robot next door.

Returning then to the normal situation, with your eyes, ears, and nose in their original positions on your head, we would have to conclude that your experience of being somewhere in the middle of your head is nothing to do with the fact that your brain is inside your skull. It comes from the fact that your primary sensing of the world comes through senses located around the head.

I say 'primary' because we also receive some data from senses distributed around the body – touch receptors in the skin, for example, and other receptors in our muscles and tendons that inform the brain of the body's position. These undoubtedly give a certain feeling of being located in the body – or rather, of being located wherever these sensory organs happen to be located – but they have far less impact on our conscious minds. The primary impact is from senses located around the head, and that is where we primarily experience ourselves to be. Somewhere behind our eyes and between our ears – that is, in the center of our head.

Where on Earth Are You?

Let us take this thought-experiment a little further. Imagine your brain were actually located on another planet. And suppose that it were linked to an exquisitely designed organic system here on Earth, complete with eyes, ears, nose, tongue, skin, hands, and feet, and with a Biological Random Access Information Network (BRAIN for short) inside your Earth-head beaming the data to your 'real' brain on the other planet. Where would you experience yourself to be?

Would you ever doubt that 'you,' the real you, were on planet Earth? Would it make any difference to your experience where in the Universe your 'real' brain was?

And supposing this mobile organic sensing station were scanning and digesting these words, as you are now, would the experience of being a self inside a body be any different from how you now feel yourself to be?

Again it would seem that the place where 'I' am is the place that my senses are located, not the place where my brain is.

Out of This World

Similar conclusions apply to more feasible experiments. Imagine that you are experiencing a virtual reality — that is a reality generated by a computer and fed to you through 'eyephones' (stereo headphones and a pair of stereoscopic miniature visual displays in front of the eyes) and a datasuit that feeds your movements back to the computer allowing it to simulate your motion through the artificial space it has created. Under such conditions you see and feel yourself to be operating in that virtual reality. Again your memory may tell you that you are 'really' where your body is. But as far as your experience is concerned you are in the virtual reality — a reality that may well be totally unlike anything in this world, a reality that does not exist in physical space and time.

To take another experience that may be familiar to some of you, imagine yourself in a sensory isolation tank. Your body is floating in water at body temperature, reducing tactile input to near zero. You are in silence and complete darkness. For as long as you remember that you are in the tank, you construct that experience around you, and 'you' remain in the tank. But after a while you forget where you are, and create a new world based on internal data your brain has generated. You no longer experience yourself to be in the tank but in the reality you have imagined. To an outside observer you are in the tank; but that is because they identify you with your body. To you who have no awareness of your body, you are where you always are – at the center of your experience.

This analysis throws a different light on so-called 'out-of-the-body experiences.' In these a person might suddenly find herself floating near the ceiling looking down on her body lying in bed. Or she may find herself at some location far from her body, across the world even. Such experiences are sometimes explained in terms of the person's consciousness having temporarily left the body. But if consciousness was never located in the body in the first place, it cannot leave it. What has happened is that the normal association of the self with the body and its senses has been broken; and, for reasons that we still do not understand, the self is now deriving its perceptual data from another location – and so experiences itself to be *at* that other location.

Nowhere

Continuing with our thought-experiments, what happens when there is no input from any senses and no data reaching consciousness from the brain or any other source?

Such situations are not at all uncommon. They occur when you are fast asleep without dreams, under an anesthetic, or deep in meditation with a silent mind. Where are you then?

You have ceased to be at the center of any sensory or imagined experience. You have temporarily ceased to be any particular where. You are literally no-where.

This does not, however, imply that you have ceased to be. The self is simply being – without the experience of being somewhere.

As we saw in the previous chapter, the deepest state of meditation, in which the mind is still, is consciousness without content. It is the self pure and simple, in its natural, unconditioned state. What our thought-experiments suggest is that this pure self has no intrinsic 'where.' In this respect 'we,' the innermost essence our consciousness, are no-where. Our daily-life experience of being located at a particular point in space is something we have created. We have taken our sensory data, from it created a perception of the world, and then, quite naturally, imagined ourselves to be at the center of it. We have created the experience of being somewhere.

Such is the power of our creativity.

When Are You?

What then of time? 'When are you?'

Again the answer might at first seem obvious: 'At this particular hour, day, and year.'

However, as we shall see in the next chapter, modern physics sees space and time simply as different aspects of the same spacetime continuum – that is, they are in essence the same thing. So what holds for our non-locatability in space must also hold for time.

Initially this may be a lot more difficult to grasp, particularly since there is such a strong time thread to our experience. But some parallel thought-experiments in the temporal domain will show that once again all is not what it seems.

Imagine, first, that your sensory nerves are connected not to TV cameras, microphones, and other artificial organs, but to a multi-track tape-recording of the electrical input that your eyes, ears, nose, and skin fed to your brain yesterday. And this is the only input your brain has. When would 'you' be? You would still experience yourself to be in the now, but when would 'now' be – the 'now' that other people observe your body to be in, or the 'now' of yesterday?

Or imagine that your brain is connected to a recording of the sensory input from someone living a hundred years ago. Where would you *experience* yourself to be? In the twentieth century or the nineteenth century?

To take the experiment one stage further, suppose that it were indeed possible to cast your mind into the future and experience the unfurling of future events. In what time would the self be? Your body may still be in this 'now,' but where and when would 'you' be?

There are also times when we have no experience of time. This can happen with a deep anesthetic. Under such conditions our consciousness is switched off to such a degree that there is no sense of any passing of time. On awakening one may feel that no time at all has elapsed since receiving the anesthetic. It can be quite disorientating.

Timeless experiences also occur in deep meditation when the

mind is still, yet awake. As it is a changeless state there is little sense of duration, no awareness of how much time has passed. One has returned to the present; and the present is discovered to be timeless.

Consciousness in its natural unconditioned state is not in time. Time does not 'pass,' nor does it have any particular location in time. It is no-when. Beyond time. But always 'now.'

As with our location in space, our experience of being at a particular moment in time is something we have created. Data from the senses – or elsewhere – has given this eternal sense of 'now' an association with a particular historical 'now.' And so we find ourselves in time.

Extra-Spatio-Temporals

We began this exploration by asking 'Where is my self?' It seemed a natural enough question. But we can now begin to see that maybe it was the wrong question. Even to ask it is to make a fundamental error. It assumes that the self is a thing – something to be described, an object of experience. 'Things' certainly have definite locations in space and time – they are part of the material creation; but the self, the experiencer of all these things, is not part of the physical world. It is not bounded by space or time.

I, the real I, is no-thing – nowhere and nowhen.

Many of us may harbor feelings that we do not quite belong here; that we are in some way alien to this world. In some respects we are all aliens. But we are not ETs – not extra-terrestrials from another planet, from another part of space, or from another time. As far as our true identity is concerned, we are aliens to both space and time. We belong nowhere and nowhen. We are potentially everywhere, and in essence nowhere; potentially eternal, and in essence nowhen.

We, the conscious entities behind our experience, are out of time, and out of space. We are not so much ETs as ESTs – extra-spatio-temporals. And as far as an EST is concerned it simply 'is.'

EMBODIMENT –
MATTER IN MIND

A person is neither a thing nor a process but an opening
or a clearing through which the Absolute can manifest.

Ken Wilber

Much as it may contradict our daily experience we do not belong to
the world of matter, space, and time. Our bodies and our sense
organs are certainly a part of that world; they are physical objects
with mass, existing at well-defined points in space and time. But
our sensations, our perceptions, our thoughts, our feelings, our
intuitions – all that occupies our awareness – are in the world of
Mind.* Mind cannot be weighed, nor, as we have just seen, can it
be located at a particular point in space and time.

I sometimes have an image of the Universe as a huge balloon.
The whole of physical creation – all matter, all the stars and
galaxies, all space and time – are inside the balloon. Outside the
balloon is the world of Mind – the world that is outside of space
and time, a world with no physical matter. The world of extra-
spatio-temporal being.

Punched through the skin of the balloon are countless tiny holes.
These holes are our senses. They are the point of connection – the
interface – between these two worlds. Through these pores the
world of Mind looks into the world of matter.

And the world It finds is a world full of form – full of shapes,
colors, sounds, smells, and sensations. A world full of things that

---

* I use Mind with a capital 'M' to designate the whole field of subjective experience, both conscious
and unconscious. This is not to be confused with another common use of the word 'mind' – that of
our thoughts and ideas as opposed to our feelings and emotions. All of these are aspects of Mind.

draw and captivate the attention. So entranced is the Mind by the richness of this experience, It forgets Itself. It forgets that It is the consciousness that is observing this world. Instead It thinks It is the particular pore in the skin through which It is peeking.

It becomes an individual mind. A mind existing within a body. A mind localized at a particular point in space and time.

Looking around, this individual mind sees other sets of senses – other pores in the skin of the balloon. It guesses that behind these other sets of senses are other minds, similar to itself. And that within each of these minds is another separate and individual self, each located at its own particular point in space and time.

These other minds in turn see it. They respond to its body and its behavior, reinforcing its belief that it *is* an individual entity living in the material world.

Somewhere in the back of its mind it retains a vague recollection that, somehow, all minds are connected. But compared to its experience of the material world this remembrance is very dim.

If this mind happens to find itself in a body that has hands or some other means with which to manipulate its surroundings, it will likely turn its attention to the task of making this world a better place – somewhere it can find peace and fulfillment.

Any faint recollection it may have had of immortality is soon forgotten. It comes to believe that the world of matter, space, and time is the only reality – or at least the only one it should be concerned with.

Time and Timelessness

To wake up is to reawaken to the world of Mind – the timeless consciousness that we in essence are.

This does not mean that the physical Universe is unreal. The world of matter, space, and time in which our bodies, brains, and sense organs exist is very real. Waking up is simply the recognition that the world of Mind – the world beyond time and space – is equally real.

Awakening is realizing that each of us exists in both realities – both in time and out of time. Our individual sense of self – the identity we derive from our interaction with the physical world – is time dependent. It exists in time along with our bodies, senses, and the many things that tell us who we are. And the pure self, the

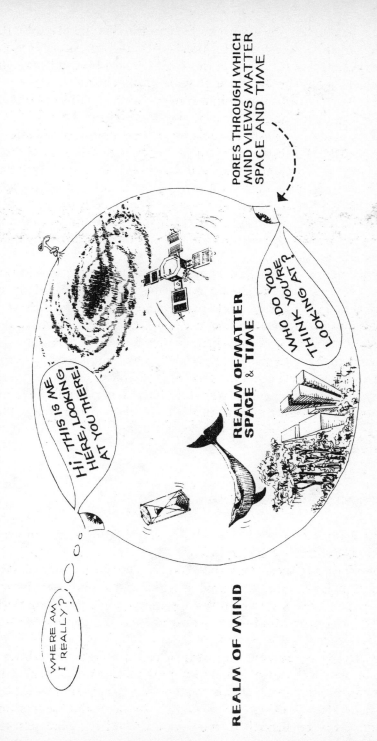

consciousness that is the ground of our very being and which is independent of our worldly experience, does not exist in time.

In short, time and timelessness are equally real. They coexist as complementary dimensions to our consciousness.

Not only is this true for our experience, it also turns out to be true in the world of physics. Here, too, time and timelessness coexist. To see just how and why, we must venture briefly into Einstein's world of relativity.

LIGHT –
A TIMELESS REALM

For the rest of my life I want to reflect on what light is.

Albert Einstein

Einstein's Special Theory of Relativity concerns the way in which space and time vary according to the speed of the observer. This, we shall see, has implications both for the reality – and unreality – of time and for our concept of 'now.'

Einstein built his theory on two revolutionary postulates. The first was that there is no absolute state of rest against which motion can be measured. In other words, all motion is relative.

As a simple example of this principle, imagine yourself standing on the ground watching a train pass by. Your experience tells you that you are at rest and the train is moving. Now imagine yourself sitting in the train. Your experience again tells you that you are at rest; this time it is the ground that is moving.

While common sense might declare that 'in reality' the train is moving and the world is at rest, Einstein argued that there is no way of verifying this. No experiment can ever prove that one frame of reference is really moving and another is really at rest. For example, imagine dropping a pebble and observing its fall. If you are standing on the ground it will fall vertically to your feet. Drop a pebble in the train and it will not slam at high speed into the end of the carriage; it will fall 'vertically' to your feet where it will stay 'at rest.'

Thus, postulated Einstein, there is no absolute state of rest. Motion can only be measured relative to other motion. And all frames of reference are equally valid.

Einstein's second postulate was that the speed of light never varies however fast you move. Imagine yourself cycling down a road at 20 m.p.h. A car traveling at 30 m.p.h. overtakes you. A bit of elementary arithmetic reveals that you would observe the car to be moving 10 m.p.h. faster than you. But some strange findings in physics led Einstein to suspect that light did not obey the same laws. He concluded that however fast you might travel, light would always pass you at the same speed – 186,000 miles per second. Even if you were traveling at 185,000 miles per second, light would still pass by 186,000 miles per second faster.

However strange it may seem, subsequent experiments have confirmed this postulate. All observers, whatever their speed, always measure the speed of light relative to them to be the same.*

There may not be many absolutes in the Universe, but the speed of light seems to be one. Light is somehow very special – completely different from everything else in the physical universe.

Slowing Time

Combining these two postulates, Einstein concluded that the faster something traveled the more slowly its clocks would run. The precise relationship between speed and time is not a straightforward one, and the actual mathematics need not bother us here. But

---

* For those who are interested, time, velocity, and the speed of light are related like the sides of a right-angled triangle. If the hypotenuse, representing the speed of light, is one unit long, the height of the triangle is the velocity (v) as a fraction of the speed of light, then the base of the triangle represents the fractional change in the rate of passing of time (t) – see figure A. In these units the relationship is simply $v2+t2=1$.

When the velocity is zero, the hypotenuse is horizontal and the time fraction is 1, i.e. it has not slowed (figure B). If the velocity is <fr⅗> the speed of light, the time has slowed by a fraction <fr⅗> (the well-known 3,4,5 triangle of figure C). And should the velocity be 1, that is equal to the speed of light, then time will have slowed to zero (figure D).

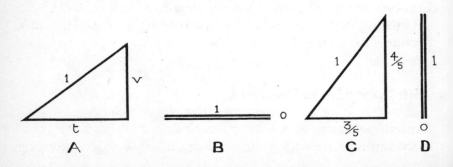

what the equations show is that if you were to travel past me at 87 percent the speed of light, I would observe your clocks to be running at half the speed of mine. This slowing applies not just to man-made clocks, but to all atomic processes, to all physical processes, to all chemical processes, and to all biological processes. Your whole world would run at half the rate of mine.

On the other hand, your point of view is as valid as mine – there is, remember, no absolute frame of reference. From your perspective it is you who are at rest and I who am moving past at high speed. You would observe that all my clocks were running at half the speed of yours.

That, you may think, does not make sense; how can each observer see the other's clocks to be running slower than their own? The theory must be wrong. But, paradoxical as it may seem, experiments have shown that the theory is correct. The reason we do not notice such strange effects in everyday life is that the speeds we experience are so small compared to the speed of light. Nevertheless, the clocks on board a 747 are running slow – by a factor of about one in a trillion.

Length and Mass

It is not just time that shrinks. Lengths measured in the direction of travel are similarly foreshortened. An object traveling at 87 percent the speed of light appears only half as long as when it is standing still.

Strange things also happen to mass. The faster things travel the heavier they appear to us who are at rest. If an object were to reach the speed of light we would observe its mass to be infinite.

To move an object of infinite mass would need an infinite amount of energy – more than there is in the entire Universe. Consequently no material object can ever reach the speed of light.

Light, of course, travels at the speed of light. This is possible because it has no mass.

The Spacetime Interval

Einstein's explorations led him to conclude that what we observe as space and time are simply different aspects of a single underlying reality – what he called 'the spacetime continuum.' Whenever we observe this continuum it appears as a particular amount of space – length, breadth, and height – and a particular amount of time; the actual proportions depending upon our speed.

Although different observers may separate the continuum into different amounts of time and space, they all agree, no matter how fast they may be moving, that the 'total' amount of spacetime separating two events – the 'interval' – is constant. I say 'total,' but space and time do not add up like simple numbers. The mathematical formula for their combination is more complex than that – something like 'space squared minus time squared.'

What the observers disagree on is how much of the spacetime interval has manifested as space, and how much has manifested as time. They are, so to speak, looking at the spacetime continuum from different perspectives; dividing it in different ways. It is a bit like cutting a string in two. People may cut a length of string in different places, but they will always end up with the same total amount of string however different the two pieces.

The World of Light

Curiouser and curiouser. . . . But even stranger things lie in store when we look at the Universe from light's point of view.

Consider the following thought-experiment – one very similar to that which Einstein himself conducted in the development of his theory. Imagine yourself to be a ray of light traveling from the Sun to the Earth. How does the Universe now look?

The equations of relativity tell us that at the speed of light, length measured in the direction of travel shrinks to nothing. And time slows to a standstill. As far as the light itself is concerned, it has traveled no distance, and taken no time to do it in.

This reflects a unique property of light. The interval between the emission of a light ray and its absorption is always zero. Or to put it another way, in the mathematical formula that combines space and time, the distance traveled by a light ray is exactly balanced by the time it takes to do it.

When we, from our earthly frame of reference, observe this zero interval, we see it as a distinct amount of space – the 93 million miles separating the Sun from us – and an 'equal' amount of time – the eight minutes it apparently takes the light to cross that distance.

But an observer moving with the light ray would see this zero interval as a zero distance and zero time.

The Speed of Light

Traveling no distance in no time, the notion of speed is meaningless for light itself. The speed of light is only meaningful to observers in the physical realm – the realm of matter in which our bodies and sensory organs are. We are the ones who observe that light travels a certain distance in a certain time – and so has speed.

What we observe as the speed of light, light observes as a ratio of manifestation. As far as it is concerned, our observation of the light has drawn its zero interval out into discrete amounts of space and time. And for every second of time that is created, 186,000 miles of space are also created.

This is why the speed of light always appears to us in the material world to be a constant 186,000 miles per second. It is a reflection of the constant relationship between space and time. It is, from light's point of view, a law of manifestation.

The Nature of Light

Not only do we in the material realm observe that light has speed, we observe that energy travels from one end of the ray to the other. And we want to know how the energy traveled. Did it travel as a wave? Or as a particle?

Strange as it may seem, it appears to be both. In some situations light behaves as a continuous wave spreading out in space – but a wave without a medium. In other situations it behaves as a particle traveling through space – but a particle without mass. Physicists have accommodated these two seemingly conflicting and paradoxical observations by deciding that light is a 'wave-particle.' In certain circumstances it appears as a wave; in others as a particle.

From light's point of view, of course, it is neither. Since it did not travel through space and time, it needed no vehicle or mechanism of travel – it has no need to be either a wave or a particle. As far as light itself is concerned, there is no duality, no paradox.

The physicist's conundrum stems from trying to model light in concepts and terms appropriate to the realm of matter. This is a world of objects with mass moving at sub-light speeds. It is a world where energy moves across space, and takes time to do it. It is a world of mechanics, quantum or otherwise. It is a world of things. This is not the world of light.

Little wonder then that our attempts to define the nature of light are confusing and self-contradictory.

The Two Realms

The world seen from light's perspective is a radically different world from that seen by all other observers. In fact, the views are so dissimilar that the Universe can be thought of in terms of two distinct realms. There is the realm of matter – a realm of space, time, and separation – the realm of sub-light speeds. And there is the realm of light, a realm that matter can never enter, a realm in which space, time, and separation take on different properties. In one realm there are waves and particles. In the other only an energy exchange. And, just as mass can never reach the speed of light, light never slows to take on the qualities of matter. They are two very separate worlds.

Even more fascinating, these two realms show parallels with the two worlds of the self that we explored in the previous chapter. There is the self that looks through the senses into the world of matter. A self that knows time. A self that experiences itself as a unique individual, living in a body. And there is the self that is outside of space and time. The pure consciousness behind all experience, nowhere and nowhen.

The question we have to ask is, how deep do these parallels run? Are they a coincidence, or do they reflect some deeper underlying unity?

NOW –
IN LIGHT AND MIND

There is a light that shines beyond all things on earth,
beyond the highest, the very highest heavens. This is the
light that shines in your heart.

Chandogya Upanishad

Light and consciousness share several things in common. One of
them concerns a central thread of our exploration – the present
moment.

As far as each ray of light is concerned it exists for only an instant
– a moment with no duration. This does not mean that time has
disappeared completely. Many events took place before the ray of
light existed, and there will be many others in the future. But the
light itself 'knows' only a single moment – a moment of now.

Likewise, our consciousness exists only in the present moment.
We may think of the past and future, but this thinking takes place in
the present. In this sense the whole of our experience exists only in
the 'now.' Now is all we ever know.

This eternal now is very different from the historical now – the
present time that we are living through. The ever-present now of
our experience is a continuous now that threads through time. It is
a now that is always with us, a fundamental quality of every
experience.

The historical now, on the other hand, is but a single instant of
experience. It is the juncture between past and future, so infini-
tesimally thin it hardly exists. It passes by us in a flash. This is the
now of clock time. It is the now in which I am sitting here, while
someone else in Australia is fast asleep, while space probes in orbit
round the Sun relay data back to Earth. It is a present moment that

we share, wherever we might be. A moment of simultaneity threaded through space.

Or so it seems. Einstein's work showed there was no such 'now' – at least not one that everyone would agree upon.

No Now

According to the Special Theory of Relativity, observers in different frames of reference – that is, observers moving at different speeds – may disagree as to the amount of time and space they see separating two events. Imagine that an astronaut on the moon sends to us a flash of light. Taking into account the time it takes the light to travel to the Earth, you could calculate the exact time at which the flash occurred on the moon. And the astronaut will agree it was indeed the moment he sent the flash. In other words, his now agrees with your now. But this is only because you both share the same frame of reference – relative to each other you are stationary.

Things are very different for an observer moving through our solar system at high speed. She sees different proportions of space and time. In her frame of reference the flash on the moon did not coincide with the moment of clock time you measured on Earth. From her perspective there is a definite time difference between these two events. They did not occur in the same moment of now.

Most of the events that you observe as simultaneous occurrences are, in her frame of reference, spread out across time. And conversely, most of her simultaneous events would seem to us to occur at different times. Since all frames of reference are equally valid, we cannot say that one view is more correct than the other. In short, there is no absolute now – no well-defined present moment stretching across the Universe.

Never and Always Now

There is a second way in which this historical sense of now is an illusion. Because of the time it takes for light to travel to my eye, I see everything as it was in the past. The page in front of me is one-trillionth of a second in the past. The Moon I see as it was a second ago, the Sun as it was eight minutes ago, the star Sirius nine years ago. And the Andromeda Galaxy (the farthest I can see with my naked eye) 2,500,000 years ago. I am seeing none of them as they are now – in the historical sense.

That is what physics tells us.

As far as my experience is concerned, however, I observe them all in the present moment. When I look up at the Sun I experience it now. I may know that I am 'in fact' seeing it eight minutes in the past, but this does not alter my experience. I still see it as now. The same is true of the book in front of me, the Moon, Sirius, and the Andromeda Galaxy; I experience them existing now.

Interestingly, this 'naïve' now of my experience is the same now as that of the light itself. As far as light is concerned the moment it left the Sun is the same moment it arrived at my eye. From its perspective there is no time interval. This coincides exactly with my experience. The realm of consciousness and the realm of light would seem to share the same experience of now.

A Mind of Light

There are other similarities between light and consciousness. Neither is an object or a thing. They are not part of the physical world. Neither of them exists in the space and time we know. And neither of them can be experienced in the same way that objects are. Both are immaterial. Both remain beyond our grasp; however fast you travel you cannot reach the speed of light, and however hard you try you cannot comprehend in worldly terms the essence of the self.

Moreover, just as physics has been reluctant to consider the Universe from light's frame of reference, giving greater reality to the world of matter – the world in which our experimental apparatus exists – so we in our own lives tend to underplay the realm of consciousness, giving greater reality to the material world we observe through our sensory apparatus.

Yet, overlooked as they may be, both are fundamental. Both are, in a sense, the source of the world. In the beginning there was light. Only as the Universe began to expand and cool were the elementary particles of matter created. In this respect matter may be thought of as 'crystallized' light; energy that has taken on the form and qualities of matter in the manner prescribed by Einstein's equation $e=mc^2$. In a parallel way, the light of consciousness is always there 'in the beginning.' It is essential for any experience. And it is, in a sense, the substance of every experience. All that we ever perceive, think, and feel are creations within the mind. They are, so to speak, 'colors' that our consciousness takes on.

In this there lies another parallel. Physics defines 'white light' as light that contains all frequencies – all the colors of the rainbow. When white light shines on an object such as a rose, certain frequencies are absorbed. Those remaining are reflected back, giving the rose its particular color. We could also consider pure consciousness as 'white' – a field of all possibilities. It is when it is colored by the senses – and by our memory and imagination – that consciousness takes on the shapes, smells, sounds, and sensations of the world we experience.

A Hole in the World

We know this inner light as the Self. This, we have seen, is not part of the world of experience. It is a hole in the fabric of space and time – a pore through which the light of the world influences the world of the mind. And it is a pore through which the light of consciousness flows into the world.

Holes are difficult to describe. In fact there is nothing to describe. They are not something so much as an absence of something. In this regard a hole in a piece of wood is, in itself, no different from a hole in a stone or a hole in the ground. But when I come to describe a hole I tend to describe it in terms of what is missing. I call it a wooden hole, or a stone hole, or a hole in the ground. In effect I am defining the hole by what it is surrounded by. I am giving holes different qualities, and thus differentiating one from another. In doing so I am making the hole into something that it is not.

Similarly with the Self, the hole in the world. Describing and defining it is very difficult. It is not so much a part of the world as a hole in the world – an absence of materiality, an absence of form, an absence of qualities. When we try to describe this Self we find no thing. And so we identify it in terms of what surrounds it – the body, feelings, personality, memories, or whatever. Thus do we make the Self into a thing – which it is not.

Thus, also, do we differentiate ourselves from one another. Yet one hole in the fabric of the world is in essence no different from any other. The pore through which I shine is intrinsically no different from the pore through which you shine. Neither is the light that shines through them any different. It is the same light in all people, in all creatures, in all conscious entities. It is the light of being itself.

Of this dimension we are, however, but dimly aware. We have become só full of our experience, so lost in the world, so caught in our attachments to whatever we think will make us feel at ease, we have overlooked the most obvious fact of our existence. Seeking fulfillment through our outer experience, we have shaped and reshaped the world to such degrees that the world may no longer be able to sustain us.

We stand on the threshold of a great awakening. And we stand on the threshold of disaster.

Which is to be our fate? Will we, through our own self-concern, destroy our world – and hence ourselves? Will our eons of evolution come to nothing?

Or will we be able to liberate ourselves from the bondage of time? Will our true identity emerge? Will we come to see the light within as easily as we do the light without? That is the challenge facing us now.

FROM NOW
TO ETERNITY

The human heart can go to the lengths of God.
Dark and cold we may be, but this
Is no winter now. The frozen misery
Of centuries breaks, cracks, begins to move;
The thunder is the thunder of the floes,
The thaw, the flood, the upstart Spring.
Thank God our time is now when wrong
Comes up to face us everywhere,
Never to leave us 'til we take
The longest stride of soul men ever took.
Affairs are now soul size.
The enterprise is exploration into God.
Where are you making for? It takes
So many thousand years to wake,
But will you wake for pity's sake?

Christopher Fry, A Sleep of Prisoners

CRISIS –
THREAT OR OPPORTUNITY?

When a seed – or an animal – or a man is ripe, it must
mature to its next phase. Or rot.

Stewart Edward White

In the second part of this book we saw how the various environmental, economic, and social problems confronting us are symp-
tomatic of a deeper underlying crisis – a crisis in our thinking,
perception, and values.

This crisis has been coming for a long time. Its seeds were sown
some fifty thousand years ago, when *Homo sapiens,* the creature with
an enlarged neocortex, began to use its complex brain in new ways.
Something different was walking on the Earth – a species whose
future was determined not by its genes so much as by its ideas. A
species that could understand the Universe in which it found itself.
A species with unprecedented creativity. So new were these developments that some anthropologists gave this species a new name,
Homo sapiens sapiens – variously translated as the 'wise human being'
or 'man that knows it knows.'

Quite naturally we turned our new capacities to the creation of a
better world for ourselves. A world in which food was plentiful and
available all year round. A world in which we could protect
ourselves from cold and rain. A world in which disease did not
strike us so young or so often. A world in which we could live long
and fulfilling lives.

We set out with the best of intentions: to reduce suffering and be
more at peace. But unwittingly we fell into assuming that the inner
needs we were now developing could be met in the same way as our
physical needs – through having or doing the right things. Not

noticing that the mind could be happy in itself, we let ourselves be seduced by the material world and by all its fruits.

The consequences of this error were at first benign. Only later, as our tools grew more powerful, did problems appear. For not only did technology amplify our ability to satisfy our physical needs, it also amplified our ability to satisfy our psychological needs – and the 'needs' of a faltering sense of self are virtually limitless.

Rapidly our burden on the world increased. And suddenly we found ourselves a threat to millions of species – including our own.

Seeing the writing on the wall, we began awakening to our responsibilities – responsibilities both for what we had done, and for what we should do.

But then, at the very time we most needed to change, we found ourselves unable to let go. Clinging to our comforts, we seemed unwilling to bear the modest *dis*comforts that would enhance our chances of survival. Too many people preferred to risk annihilation rather than give up their attachments and illusions.

So we watched the living Earth erode – and wondered how humanity could continue to be so crazy.

The crisis that had been brewing for millennia was upon us.

Crises as Drivers

Crises are generally seen as undesirable; they imply danger and potential misfortune. There are good reasons for this. A crisis is a sign that the old ways are no longer working. In such times there can be very real danger; if appropriate responses are not made rapidly, then the old order may begin to collapse.

This is all too possible with humanity today. If we do not address the deeper psychological issues underlying the many problems we face, it is very likely that civilization will fall apart.

On the other hand, any crisis, big or small, personal or planetary, also presents an opportunity – something the ancient Chinese seemed well aware of. Their word for crisis, *wei-chi*, is written as a combination of two characters, one meaning 'danger,' the other 'opportunity.' The opportunity may not always be easy to see, but it is always there. It is the chance to remedy what was wrong and move on to a new way of being.

In this respect crises are a challenge – the challenge to recognize what is no longer working and seize the opportunity to learn, make changes, and progress. As such, crises can play an important role in development.

Evolutionary Crises

This is very apparent when we look back at the history of evolution. In the chapter entitled 'Freedom' we considered the early planetary crisis that occurred as simple bacteria began running short of food – the first of many food crises. The response to this crisis was a new way of obtaining energy – photosynthesis.

Over the next billion and a half years oxygen – the 'poisonous' by-product of photosynthesis – accumulated in the atmosphere until eventually it threatened to extinguish life on Earth. Life responded to this crisis with the evolution of a new type of cell, one that could feed on oxygen.

Later, as cells grew larger, they faced a different sort of food crisis. If a cell's diameter doubled, its surface area quadrupled while its volume increased eightfold. To keep this larger volume fed, the cell's walls had to absorb nutrients twice as fast. The larger cells grew, the more difficult it became for them to feed themselves. Another crisis, another danger, and another sign that something new was called for. The response this time was the multicellular organism – cells stayed the same size, but the organism of which they were part was free to grow.

Today, life on Earth has arrived at another crisis. The values that have guided its dominant species throughout most of its development are no longer working. Preservation of the self may have been very valuable in prehistoric times. It may also have been valuable when the world was a collection of independent communities and states – although, even then, self-centeredness among those in power often led to greed, exploitation, and corruption. But now, in the closing days of the twentieth century, such values have become positively dangerous. We live in an interconnected world. Our planet-wide communication networks are reminding us that we are one human family. Increasing economic interdependence means that changes in one area of the world have significant impact across the globe. Waste from one country drifts through the air and sea destroying food chains thousands of miles away. And the power at our fingertips is now so great that an idea in one person's head can change the world for everyone.

A new situation is at hand. And the old mode of consciousness is no longer appropriate.

Once again there is great danger. And once again Life is being driven to respond. One way or another, the old way – our outdated egocentric thinking – has to go.

Saving Ourselves

One solution would be for the human race to go. Despite what many people appear to believe, Gaia – the name given to the Earth as a living organism – does not need us to save her. She would probably recover much better without us.

Indeed, she might even hasten our departure. A new and virulent virus, for example, would do quite well. It would simply be Gaia's immune system responding to a dangerous cancer. Alternatively, what we call 'the greenhouse effect' may, for the planet, be merely a fever whose function is to eliminate this dangerous creature.

If humanity were suddenly to disappear, it would not be long before grass was growing over our highways. In a few hundred years most of our buildings would have returned to dust and rubble. Those that remained a while longer would be treated like any other rock and become a home for mosses, lichens, bears, and eagles. Atmospheric visibility would soon be back to a hundred miles, and within ten thousand years carbon dioxide levels would be returning to normal. A few isolated sore spots might remain. Some dumps of toxic waste could stay barren for a hundred thousand years; a few more deserts might be created as the last remnants of topsoil blew off the more impoverished land. But within a few million years Gaia would have replenished her diverse stock of species. Little trace would remain of humanity's brief but disturbing existence.

That's if we went now. If we stayed a little longer we might destroy critical elements of the biosphere. In that case the Earth could take more time to recover.

When people talk of 'saving the planet,' most are not talking just about ensuring the continuation of life on Earth. If this were their aim, our collective suicide would be high on their agenda. Most want to save the planet in order that humanity may continue.

Before we set about saving ourselves, however, we should first ask what it is that we are trying to save. Are we trying save humanity as it is now? If so, any salvation will be short-lived. It would not be long before our dysfunctional thinking led to further crises and to further threats of extinction.

If we are truly to save ourselves, we need to do more than just save our biological selves. We must save our inner selves – save ourselves from our egocentric mode of consciousness. It is this that has to go.

A New Species

This is the real opportunity nestling within our global crisis: the opportunity to develop a new consciousness, a new way of seeing, and a new way of thinking. What is being called for is a new sub-species. A species that can manage the creativity of *Homo sapiens sapiens* with true wisdom – a *Homo sapiens sapiens sapiens*.*

This could be the new evolutionary adaptation waiting to emerge. Not, as we have seen, a biological adaptation – there is no time for that, and even if we could genetically re-engineer ourselves, it would not hit at the heart of the problem. What the crisis is driving us towards is inner change – a transformation into truly wise human beings, a species no longer fettered by self-centeredness.

It is driving us towards a new perception of ourselves; a new sense of purpose; a new way of being. We are being urged to awaken from our dream.

---

* A term suggested by Jonathan Weiner in his book *The Next One Hundred Years* – a book that could be usefully read by anyone who does not believe humanity is in deep trouble.

APOCALYPSE –
THE CHALLENGES TO COME

The world, as we know it, is coming to an end. The
world as the center of the universe, the world divided
from the heavens, the world bound by horizons in
which love is reserved for the members of the in group:
that is the world that is passing away. Apocalypse does
not point to a fiery Armageddon but to the fact that our
ignorance and our complacency are coming to an end.

Joseph Campbell

The various manifestations of our crisis have not yet forced us to
explore their underlying cause. When there is a disaster – an oil
spill, a bank crash, a nuclear accident, a crop failure, or an industrial
tragedy – we still treat each in isolation. We regret that it occurred
and do our best to clear up the mess. Not recognizing the inner
malaise that lies at the root of these disasters – the word comes from
'dis-astra,' and originally meant 'out of touch with the stars' – we
continue treating only the symptoms of the problem. We are like a
doctor who lances the boils on a patient's skin without stopping to
ask what is causing them.

These symptoms will not suddenly go away. More than likely
they will continue to become increasingly severe. We are reaping
the consequences of many years of misguided thinking, of decisions
made through self-centered and materialist value systems. Moreover, as we continue along our mistaken path we will probably find
ourselves facing economic, environmental, and social catastrophes
that make Chernobyl, Bhopal, and the Exxon Valdez seem tame. As
the refrain goes: 'You ain't seen nothing yet!'

We may actually need these growing catastrophes. The disasters we have experienced to date have not alerted us to the underlying errors in our minds – at least not enough of us to make much difference. Louder alarm bells will be necessary if we are to awaken from our slumbers. Indeed, our culture may have to be shaken at its roots before we come to our senses.

Millennial Fever

Prophecies of disaster are not new. Throughout history there have been dire warnings of the tragedies that would befall humanity, and even of the end of the world.

Various dates have been proposed for these ultimate catastrophes. Many thought the turn of the first millennium, A.D.1000, would be the end. The twelfth-century Cistercian abbot, Joachim of Flora, thought it would come in the year 1200, while others focussed on similar round dates. Hardly a century has turned without large numbers of people prophesying that the end was nigh. It is not therefore surprising to find many contemporary prophecies focussing around the year 2000.

Why then should we take current warnings any more seriously than previous ones? All earlier forecasts of doom have failed to materialize, what reason is there to suppose that current ones will be any different?

No reason. Except that coincidentally the global crisis has now come upon us. Never before in human history have the dangers been so acute, nor the likelihood of catastrophe so real. Never before has the welfare of the planet's biosystem been at stake. Danger seems to be coming from all sides at once. Suddenly we have very good reason to wonder whether we will make it past the turn of the millennium.

Moreover, the closer we come to the year 2000 the hotter things will get. If there ever was a justification for millennial fever it is now.

Apocalypse Now?

Many historical prophecies herald events that do bear a remarkable resemblance to the times we are passing through and the dangers we face. Take, for example, the centuries-old prophecy of the North

American Hopi Indians. They foresaw the coming of the white man from the East; his inventions of carriages that need no horses; and his ability to travel along roads in the sky. One part of the Hopi prophecy seems to predict World War II; another matches well with the setting up of the United Nations; while others detail the death and destruction that the white man would bring, and his desecration of the land. There are also possible allusions to nuclear weapons – 'a gourd of ashes' that would fall from the sky, boiling the oceans and burning the land so that nothing would grow for many years. This would be the signal that the final stage was approaching. Man would travel to the moon, and build a city in the sky, but then go no further.

At the height of his foolishness great wisdom returns, coming from the East. If man listens to the wisdom there will come a conscious transformation and rebirth of humanity; if not, there follows the ending of all life. This last part is particularly worth noting. The Hopi prophecy does not foretell a fixed future, but a future in which we have choice – and that choice involves a spiritual change.

This idea that wisdom will come from the East is also found in Tibetan Buddhism. In the eighth century Padma Sambhava prophesied that 'when the iron bird flies in the sky and the horses run on wheels, the Dharma [the teaching] will move to the West.'

The Judeo-Christian tradition contains several similar predictions. The Old Testament books of Samuel, Elijah, Amos, Jeremiah, Ezekiel, Habakkah, Isaiah, and Joel all foretell troubled times to come. The latter two, for example, both speak of the coming 'Day of the Lord' when the land is laid desolate and the sky so darkened that neither Moon nor Sun can be seen. Could this be a description of nuclear holocaust, the torching of oil fields, or some other environmental catastrophe?

In the New Testament we find Christ on the Mount of Olives foretelling a time when there would be many wars and rumors of wars, famines, pestilence, and earthquakes, and that the powers of Urania would be shaken. Such events would be the sign that this age was coming to a close. Whether or not the number of earthquakes has increased in recent times is not clear; but certainly there are more new wars per year than ever before; famines hit with increasing severity; new pestilences strike fear deep into the heart of individuals and insurance companies alike; and the power of uranium has certainly been shaken loose.

Such correlations are seen by many as a sign that the 'Day of Judgment' is indeed nigh, and that, to quote Christ, the generation that sees these events 'will not pass until all these things have happened.' In other words, when things start to heat up they will do so rapidly. But we should also remember that when Christ warned of future troubles, religious persecution, false prophets, and imposters claiming to be the risen Christ, he was speaking not of the end of the world, but of 'the pains of birth.' There would, he claimed, be light on the other side.

The Revelation of St. John

These prophecies bear a close resemblance to the Apocalypse – the word originally meant 'Revelation' – of St. John. In this final book of the New Testament, John gives a detailed account of various events that would herald the final day of judgment.

He tells of a scroll with seven seals representing the retributions that must come. The first four release the famous horsemen bringing war, famine, disease, and death. There are the seven angels with seven trumpets each foretelling disaster. The third of these speaks of 'wormwood' falling from the sky, turning the waters bitter and killing many people – a prophecy that makes you think when you consider that the Russian word 'Chernobyl' can be translated as 'wormwood.' Other trumpets bring warnings that sound suspiciously warlike, the Sun and Moon again becoming hidden from view.

Seven bowls are poured out: ugly and painful sores, lifeless seas, the shedding of blood, scorching by the sun, darkness, deserts, and an earthquake like never before. Again it is not hard to think of the possible fulfillment of such predictions in the contemporary world.

Then follow many other events, including the appearance of the Antichrist. This is a secular savior. He offers the hope of peace on Earth by claiming to be able to resolve the problems of the world. Not recognizing him for what he is, people rally to his call and his influence spreads into all nations.

The Antichrist's promises are, however, empty. Wars continue to proliferate, taking humanity to the brink of annihilation. Then in the final conflict – the battle of Armageddon – Christ returns and the Antichrist is finally defeated. Christ's kingdom reigns and the gospel spreads across the Earth.

Revisioning Armageddon

Most spiritual scriptures have several levels of interpretation. There is the surface meaning, the literal everyday level of interpretation; and there are other deeper meanings, metaphors for spiritual truths. The Revelation of St. John is no exception.

As has been stated earlier, we are all to some extent hypnotized by our prevailing culture into believing that our salvation lies in the material world, in what we have or do. It is this that underlies much of our egocentricity and malignant behavior patterns. Yet there remains within each of us an unhypnotized aspect. This is our natural mind, the part of our selves that knows that our inner fulfillment does not depend on the world of the senses. It is our inner guide, waiting quietly to help us when we turn to it. It is also a state of inner peace, in which there is no judgment and in which we know the real nature of love. It is the part of us that is in the present moment. It is our true reality.

If the Revelation of St. John were to be considered metaphorically as well as literally, 'Christ' would symbolize this inner source of wisdom. The dependent and conditioned mode of thought – the ego-mind – would then be symbolized by the 'Antichrist.' It is that aspect of ourselves that stands against our inner knowing – it is anti-'the Christ within.'

This mode of thinking does not wish to hear that our inner well-being is not at the mercy of the world around. Its role is to keep us bound to the material world, to all the things it tells us will bring fulfillment. It is the part of us that judges other people in terms of good or bad, ally or enemy; that blames others for our own distress; that fears the world may not give us what we want. It is the self that is caught up in the past and future.

This error in our own minds could be the 'secular savior.' It would have us believe that by correcting the errors of the world we will find the peace we seek. This false prophet cannot let us see that it is itself the error we must correct. Instead it claims it is our true self and the supreme judge of what is right and wrong.

This is 'Satan in disguise,' the prophet of material salvation that lives within us all. It is the call of the ego-mind to which the world today has rallied. And its influence has indeed spread into all nations and into all our affairs.

Yet the promises of this secular savior are empty. However much wealth and worldly success we gather, true peace of mind remains as elusive as ever. Wars continue to proliferate, taking humanity to the brink of annihilation.

But now, as the writing on the wall accumulates, we are beginning to awaken to the real nature of the conflict we are fighting – the final battle each of us must fight. It is the inner Armageddon, the battle between our ego-mind and our higher self. It is the conflict that each of us is engaged in every day. The battle between judgment and letting go, between fear and love, between our conditioning and our inner truth.

As Pogo said in the Walt Kelly comic strip, 'We have met the enemy and he is us.' It is within each and every one of us. And so is the wisdom that can see us through. We are not facing each other on different sides of the battle. We are each on both sides, each facing ourselves.

The good news is that St. John foresees the battle of Armageddon being won by Christ – suggesting that our higher knowing will eventually defeat the Antichrist within. Then Christ's kingdom reigns. This we might interpret as a world freed from the dictates of our ego-mind, a world in which a liberated mind is the norm rather than the exception, a world in which love not fear is the prevailing emotion.

There will, at last, be peace on Earth – the inner peace we have been seeking all along.

RENAISSANCE –
A SPIRITUAL IMPERATIVE

The only devils in this world are those running around in
our own hearts, and that is where all our battles should
be fought.

Mahatma Gandhi

We know that more enlightened modes of consciousness are
possible, for we have seen many examples – St. Theresa, St. Francis,
Gandhi, and the many other 'saints' and liberated souls who have
demonstrated it in their lives. And we know this liberation is not
that far away. Many of us have at times experienced what it means
simply to be oneself, secure in one's own existence: those moments
when, for one reason or another, the mind suddenly falls back into
its natural state – a state of ease.

We also know this shift need not take time. The error is only an
error of attitude and perception. These are of our own creation, and
we can change them if we choose. Indeed, a change of mind can
happen overnight – or even quicker.

What we do not know is how to allow this ease to fall upon us.
Caught up in all our doing, we assume this release must involve
some other form of doing. But it is an undoing that is required – an
undoing of the constraints we have placed upon ourselves. Yet, so
concerned have we become with how things might or might not be,
we keep ourselves in a state of disease.

We are caught in a vicious circle, and the essence of our challenge
is how to break free from it. How do we let self-liberation, which
has hitherto been the exception, become the norm?

A Spiritual Renaissance

Helping people reconnect with this state of inner ease and grace has been the underlying goal of most religious teachings. But it is also clear that contemporary religion does not – in the majority of cases – do this very effectively. Many may well feel better for following a particular tradition; some may behave more charitably; and many may believe that they are saved through their faith. Nevertheless true self-liberation still remains a great rarity.

We have religion without spiritual awakening.

One reason for this is that most religions have lost touch with their source. Over the years they have collected various additions and changes that have distracted from or confused their original message. Teachings that were once intended to liberate us from our attachments have turned into belief systems – and thus into new attachments. In most instances religion has become part of our social hypnosis, not a release from it.

In addition the practices themselves, without which no spiritual teaching can be alive, have become distorted or lost. This is inevitable. It is the entropy of information, the slow inevitable decay of knowledge as it picks up random noise.

I am not therefore suggesting that we need a revival of any classical religion – or, for that matter, any new religion. In the hands of the ego-mind religion can become the most dangerous force on Earth.

What I am arguing for is a spiritual renaissance. We must find again the wisdom that originally shone through the great religions, the wisdom that illumined the minds of the great saints and sages. And we need to put this perennial philosophy of human consciousness in the language of our times, in the expressions and forms appropriate to the latter days of the twentieth century – and to the third millennium.

Practiceable Paths

Earlier we considered some everyday doorways to self-liberation – the doorways of our relationships, forgiveness, and meditation. There are, needless to say, numerous other paths to self-transcendence. Not all of them are easy. Some may be arduous and time-consuming, some may be only for particular types of people or for minds already used to discipline. Some may be dangerous without proper supervision. And some may not work very well at all.

Yet within these various techniques and teachings there may be others that are easy to disseminate, simple to practice, and quick to take effect. At present there is no general agreement on which approaches offer the best opportunities for liberation, which are most appropriate for whom, or how they may be developed and improved. All that is certain is that no existing path has so far succeeded in transforming humanity as a whole.

The absence of such a path does not imply that it does not exist. It could lie buried in some process known only to a few. It could be staring us in the face in some practice of meditation whose value has not yet been widely appreciated. It could lie in the synergy of several existing approaches. Or it could be in some process yet to be discovered.

An Inner Manhattan Project

The crisis is acute, and time is running very short. If we are to win our inner Armageddon we must do more than hope – or pray – that we will wake up in time. Humanity needs to make a collective and concerted effort to accelerate its inner evolution.

Perhaps we need the inner equivalent of the 'Manhattan Project.' This, as some may recall, was the code name given to the development of an atomic bomb. So urgent was this task seen to be, that vast scientific, technical, and financial resources were pumped into the project. For the first time in history, a variety of universities and technical institutions across the U.S.A. worked on the same endeavor – and within three years the first atomic bomb had been detonated. With hindsight we may well question the wisdom of this development; nevertheless the project did show how much we can achieve once we put our minds to it.

Today the urgency is no less – on the contrary, it is even greater. We are facing the headlong rush of humanity towards disaster. If we really want to survive – and want our children and our children's children to survive – it is essential that we put our minds to the task of raising our consciousness. We need nothing short of a world-wide effort to liberate humanity from the destructive grip of its self-centeredness – a global 'R and D' program to enlighten the species – an 'Inner Manhattan Project.'

Such a project would entail research and development not in new material technologies so much as in inner technologies – technologies that promote psychological maturation and inner awakening. Items on its agenda could include: a greater focus on neurosciences and psychology; understanding the nature of mind; exploring the roots of our self-centeredness in more depth; a global audit of existing paths of spiritual development; the search for new approaches; the synthesis of existing practices; and, equally important, the application and dissemination of its discoveries.

Being relatively low technology, an Inner Manhattan Project would not involve the huge amounts of money we currently pour into fighting our material wars. Far less than 1 percent of the trillion dollars the world spends each year on 'defense' would do quite handsomely.

SETBACK – A HISTORY OF CONSTRUCTIVE EXTINCTIONS

... but as when
The bird of wonder dies, the maiden phoenix,
Her ashes new-create another heir
As great in admiration as herself.

William Shakespeare

The possibility that humanity may not pass the test that Life has set cannot be overlooked. The pathways to failure are both numerous and diverse. We are facing a range of environmental dangers – and there are probably many more of which we are still unaware. The stress of ever-increasing change could also have disastrous consequences – remember, 80 percent of 'accidents' are caused by human error. Nor can we ignore the dangers of war. As resources become less plentiful and social tensions increase, wars of one kind or another become evermore likely; and the weaponry now at our fingertips can destroy ecosystems as easily as people. A nuclear holocaust would be an environmental disaster.

Any catastrophe – 'natural' or otherwise – that destroyed the infrastructure of contemporary civilization could send humanity into a new Dark Age. Serious as that might seem to us, it would be a relatively minor setback for evolution.

The consequences would be much more serious if, for instance, the greenhouse effect were to become a runaway reaction. It would not be just coastal cities and farmlands that were ruined; the regional ecologies critical for the survival of millions of species would be destroyed. This could result in evolution being set back millions of years.

Worse still, if a significant proportion of the ozone layer were destroyed, the ultraviolet light that streamed in from space could make the land uninhabitable. Once again life would be confined to the sea – a setback of 350 million years.

The Demise of the Dinosaur

Such setbacks are not new to evolution. A major disaster occurred 66 million years ago when the dinosaurs' reign came to an abrupt end. And it was not just the dinosaurs that died; millions of other species, both plant and animal, suddenly became extinct.

Exactly what caused this catastrophe is still not certain. That it was some form of environmental change is pretty clear. The sedimentary rock that forms the boundary between the time of the dinosaurs, the Cretaceous Era, and the Tertiary Era that followed consists of a thin layer of clay. Samples of this clay taken around the world show between a hundred and ten thousand times the normal level of soot. This suggests a colossal, planet-wide fire, during which a major proportion of the planet's forests went up in smoke. Supporting evidence comes from the unusual abundance of nitrogen isotopes in this layer; this could have come from heavy acid rain. Another consequence of widespread fire would have been an increase in carbon dioxide, perhaps triggering a greenhouse effect.

Clues as to how such a fire might have started can be found in the high levels of iridium in this clay. Iridium is a rare element on Earth; but is not so rare in meteors. This, along with the discovery that mineral grains in this layer show signs of intense shock, suggests that a large meteor, perhaps several miles in diameter, struck the Earth – and there is strong evidence for at least one very large impact occurring around that time.

As well as starting widespread fires, such an impact would have produced massive clouds of dust. The result could have been very similar to a 'nuclear winter.' Many plants would have been eliminated, destroying important elements in the food chain – at the top of which sat the dinosaurs.

Other researchers have proposed that volcanoes were the cause. Volcanic dust contains high levels of iridium and produces similar layers of clay. And the shock waves from both volcanoes and earthquakes can result in comparable stresses in crystals. Furthermore, there is geological evidence of an intense period of volcanic activity around that time, which could well have thrown huge plumes of fiery ash and gases into the upper atmosphere.

It is very possible that both these hypotheses are correct. The impact of a very large meteor could have smashed a hole through the continental crust, exposing the Earth's mantle of red-hot, semi-molten rock. This could easily have triggered a series of massive volcanic eruptions.

Or perhaps some other series of events was to blame. During the million or so years immediately preceding the dinosaurs' demise the climate seems to have undergone a series of significant changes. Possibly some phenomenon that we do not yet know about was the trigger – fifty years ago we knew nothing of the greenhouse effect. All that is certain is that a large proportion of the species disappeared in a relatively short period of time.

Past Extinctions

The end of the Cretaceous Era was but one of a series of mass extinctions. Over the life of this planet there have been at least seven other times when the number of species fell suddenly and dramatically. Two hundred and thirteen million years ago the Triassic Era came to an abrupt end – again with signs of intense shock. (At about the same time a large meteor created the forty-mile Manicouagan crater in Quebec.)

Two hundred and forty-eight million years ago another mass extinction resulted in the loss of 90 percent of all species then living, ending the Permian Era of Earth's history.

A hundred million years before that the Devonian Era ended in a mass extinction of marine life. (Again the sedimentary rock from the time shows an unusually high level of iridium.)

Around 440 million years ago three close periods of extinction associated with a major global glaciation and lowering of sea level brought an end to the Ordovician Era. Before that, other major extinctions occurred 500, 570, and 630 million years ago. And there may well have been others of which we are as yet unaware.

Mass Extinction Now

Today we are experiencing in slow motion the start of another mass extinction. This time, however, it is not meteors or volcanoes that are responsible but one of the Earth's own creatures.

Before the appearance of humanity there were more species on the planet than at the time of the dinosaurs – a remarkable recovery whose significance we shall return to shortly. But as soon as human beings appeared things began to change. In our early days we hunted to extinction some of the large animals in North and South America and parts of Africa. Later we eradicated many species simply because they were in our way. And more recently we have destroyed many more through sheer lack of care.

Currently species are disappearing at the rate of one an hour! At this rate half of the Earth's plant and animal species will have been eliminated within the next few hundred years. But, given that our destructive potential accelerates along with our technological 'progress,' we will probably reach this point much sooner.

On the graph of extinctions we have already fallen over the precipice. The entire history of humanity occupies less than a thousandth of an inch along the time axis of the graph on page 189. And our own lifetimes correspond to less than a millionth of an inch on this scale. Yet they have resulted in a drop in the curve that is very clearly visible.

But the curve need not plummet further. We have not yet entered a full-blown greenhouse effect. The ozone layer is still intact. Not all the forests have been destroyed. We need not become, like the dinosaurs, a species that suddenly disappeared – a mere geological relic. There is still hope. We still have the opportunity to redeem ourselves.

Evolutionary Kicks

Even if another mass extinction were to occur, all would not be lost. Evolution would still continue. Indeed, if the past is anything to go by, it would leap ahead.

Hard-bodied organisms only began to flourish after the mass marine extinction that ended the Pre-Cambrian Era. Amphibians only began to colonize the land after the Devonian extinction 365 million years ago. And it was the major extinction of 248 million years ago that preceded the appearance of the first dinosaurs.

The catastrophe that ended the dinosaurs' reign led in turn to the evolution of mammals. Small, rodent-like mammals did already exist, but had not evolved very fast. However, the fact that some of them lived in burrows probably helped them survive whatever environmental catastrophe befell those times. Afterwards they evolved very rapidly, diversifying into the wealth of mammal species that we now know – including ourselves.

The reason for this sudden burst of evolutionary activity is easy to understand. Before the catastrophe the ecological system would have been in a stable state; most species would have had plenty of time to become well adapted to their environment. There would have been little pressure for evolutionary change.

After a mass extinction things would have been very different. The living matrix of the biosphere would have changed profoundly. Most species that survived would have found themselves in circumstances to which they were not so well suited – sources of food might have disappeared, the climate might have changed, new dangers might have emerged. In this new ecological context, life would have been under renewed pressure to evolve. New adaptations would establish themselves fast and new species would proliferate.

In short, the curve of evolution would have leapt upward once more.

The Upside of Extinction

Mass extinctions can therefore have a positive side. If the dinosaurs had not disappeared when they did, mammals might have remained as rodents and human beings would never have been born. In this respect we have good reason to be thankful for the disaster of 66 million years ago.

And, should it turn out that humanity's activities do result in another decimation of the planet's species, who is to say what new evolutionary opportunities this might create? The dinosaurs would never have guessed that mammals, human beings, and civilization would follow them. Who knows what phoenix could arise from our ashes?

Whatever form they might take, the species that followed our demise might be very thankful to us for having set the stage and for creating the evolutionary opportunity it needed.

Who knows, they might even thank us for the genetic modifications that our nuclear and biological industries left in their wake.

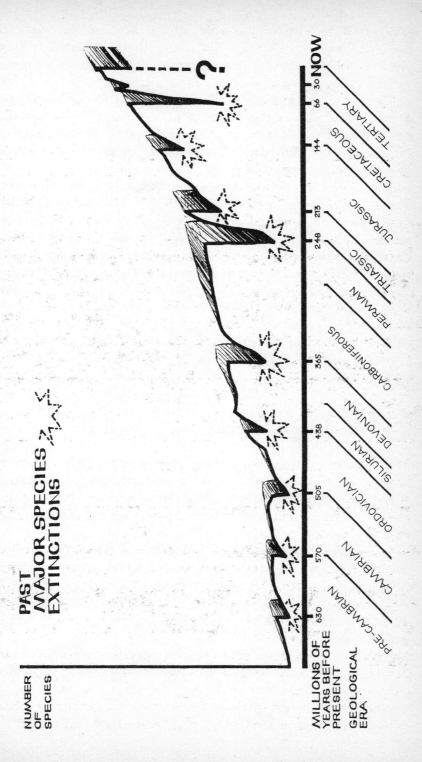

Knocking on Heaven's Door

Whatever happens one thing is certain. However much life on Earth may be set back, evolution will continue its steady march towards greater complexity and higher order.

If we were to set ourselves back fifty thousand years to some 'New Stone Age,' our rate of development would be slowed considerably. But it would not stop accelerating. We would once again strive to improve our lot, and each new advance we made would serve as a platform for further advances. The feedback cycle would continue as before.*

Moreover, although such a calamity might set us back considerably in our material progress, our internal progress would not be so badly affected. It seems probable that we would retain much of the knowledge, understanding, learning, and awareness that we have accumulated. We would have a head start over our Stone Age predecessors and might well find ourselves entering a new technological age in centuries rather than millennia – though hopefully with more wisdom than before.

Even if some environmental holocaust were to wipe us out completely, genetic evolution would continue. Inevitably, but slowly, change would occur. New adaptations would arise and new species emerge. New qualities and abilities would appear – some possibly unknown to us – each serving as platforms for further evolutionary advance. Slowly but surely evolution would continue its inexorable acceleration.

Given the evolutionary trend towards higher orders of information processing, it is very likely that creatures with large and complex nervous systems would again emerge. Eventually beings with an intelligence similar to, or surpassing, our own might appear. Almost certainly such beings would develop symbolic language through which to share their discoveries, and – if they were to have some way of influencing their environment – science

---

* It is possible that humanity suffered major setbacks earlier in its history. At the end of the last ice age, some ten thousand years ago, sea levels rose by some 300 feet. Many of the human settlements of the time would have been in low-lying areas – it is warmer lower down, and easier to grow crops in river valleys than on the sides of mountains. As the waters rose these settlements would have been buried beneath the waves and their occupants forced to move to much higher ground.

Could this be the source of the myth of the Great Flood to be found in so many cultures? Could this have been what happened to the fabled Atlantis? If so, archaeologists are digging in the wrong place – they should be digging 300 feet under the sea, out on the edge of the continental shelves.

MINOR SETBACK

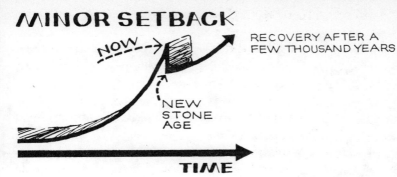

NOW ->

NEW STONE AGE

RECOVERY AFTER A FEW THOUSAND YEARS

TIME

MAJOR SETBACK

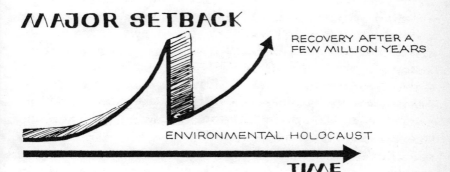

RECOVERY AFTER A FEW MILLION YEARS

ENVIRONMENTAL HOLOCAUST

TIME

REPEATED SETBACKS

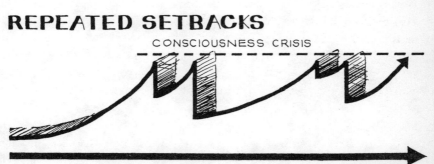

CONSCIOUSNESS CRISIS

TIME

and technology. Once more life would be caught in an ever-dizzier spiral of development.

If such beings remained stuck in a self-centered mode of consciousness, life on Earth would again come under increasing pressure. The planet would be in another crisis – another crisis of consciousness. And, if this species could not raise its level of awareness, evolution might again be thrown back another fifty thousand, or even fifty million, years.

Once more it would resume its relentless climb towards higher levels of organization, and higher rates of change. And once more it would face an inner challenge.

Again and again life would be confronted by the same challenge. Again and again it faces that test of intelligence. Again and again it must answer the same crucial questions. Is this a creature that can cope with yet greater rates of change? Is this a being that can awaken to its inner world as fully as it has to the world around? Is this an entity that can make the leap into a new age of evolution – a higher order of intelligence?

The question we have to ask is: Are we that species? Are we ready to make that leap? Can we use our gifts of understanding, creativity, and choice in our true self-interest? Can we use our growing freedom to liberate our minds?

And if we do, what lies ahead? It turns out that it may not be quite what we expect. Indeed, it may be very different from anything we have ever dared expect.

COMPRESSION –
THE COLLAPSE OF TIME

'Now! Now!' cried the Queen. 'Faster! Faster!'

Lewis Carroll

Let us suppose that humanity survives these critical times and continues to evolve. What might the future look like then?

If we survive it will be because we have come to our senses. Freed from outdated mental programs, we would find ourselves in a world where inner maturity was valued more than status and security. Apparent threats to our inner well-being would be seen for what they are – illusions. No longer ruled by fear and the dreamworld of the ego, greed and materialism would wane. Peace, both with ourselves and our environment, would at last become possible.

As to the actual way of life in such a world, very little can be said. The foundations of human culture would have changed dramatically; yet any forecasts we might venture would be heavily biased towards the realities we know today. It is rather like asking our Stone Age ancestors to imagine life in the high-tech information society of the late twentieth century – except that we are now considering a world not thousands of years in the future but mere decades ahead.

No Limits to Mind

Whatever form a society of liberated minds might take, one thing seems certain. The pace of change will continue to quicken. Breakthroughs will continue to beget breakthroughs, leading to ever-shorter intervals between new developments and evermore rapid growth.

This does not imply that material progress will continue to accelerate. The resources of this planet are finite; they present clear limits to physical growth. And as these limits are approached, the rate of growth will begin to slow. This is a common pattern in Nature. Bacteria growing in a dish will at first multiply exponentially; but as the boundaries of the dish make themselves felt the growth slows down and eventually stops. The human population is already feeling the constraints of its finite environment, and its growth is beginning to tail off. Likewise, decreasing resources and the problems of increased waste will serve as a brake on our material development.

Such limits do not herald the end of all development, only of our current mode of development – that of material technological development. We are now being called to move into a new phase of evolution – that of inner unfolding. If we make that step then growth will continue, but in a different arena. Its focus will have shifted from the realm of matter to the realm of mind.

Inward Acceleration

There is no reason why our minds should be subject to the same limits as our material development. Indeed, there a number of reasons to believe that the evolution of consciousness will occur much faster.

In the first place, inner evolution would represent another step in the direction of ephemeralization – the trend towards doing more with less matter. Just as it takes less matter and energy to modify a piece of computer software than it does to modify a piece of hardware, it takes even less to change our thinking.

The impediments to inner change are not physical but mental. They are our attitudes, our mental habits, our mindsets as to what is possible and what is right. These are generally self-imposed. As we learn how to release our minds from their attachments, we could find ourselves changing very fast indeed – in the twinkling of an eye. If we so choose.

A second factor promoting an internal acceleration is the increasing connectivity of humanity. Whether it be the joining of cells in sexual reproduction, the connection of organs through a complex nervous system, or the linkage of human beings through language, increasing connectivity has always led to greater novelty and more rapid development. The ultra-connectivity now manifesting in our global telecommunications is no exception. Television, video, audio recordings, CD-ROMs, computer networks, books, magazines, faxes, telephones, and teleconferencing can be used to share our realizations and inner awakenings. We no longer have to learn the art of liberation through a somewhat 'hit and miss' approach; we can learn from each other how best to move towards a more mature mode of being.

This means that we could expect to see new positive-feedback loops emerging. The more that we awakened from our dreams and became less attached to our imagined needs, the more free we would be to follow our higher aspirations. The better we could be of service to each other . . . and the more rapidly we would awaken.

As this positive feedback accelerates, we could find that processes that now take a lifetime could happen in years. The more that adults awoke from their dreams, the less would children be hypnotized into the erroneous thinking that is the basis of our spiritual malaise. Not having so much to unlearn as their parents, they could reach psychological maturity much quicker. Already there are signs of this: the perceptions and values of some teenagers can put the most liberated parents to shame.

The mass media could also play a vital role in augmenting this positive feedback. We have seen the role they play in perpetuating our current set of values. But if our values evolved – if we no longer laid so much emphasis on material fulfillment – the media could play a significant role in furthering humanity's inner liberation.

Who knows, perhaps there could be a higher purpose to television. More than simply a technology that allows us 'to see at a distance,' it could become a means to bring the world new vision. Guided by a less material set of values, it could help us see beyond our more mundane realities and so appreciate our true potential. Then humanity could awaken very rapidly indeed.

Liberated Creativity

Finally, we should not forget the impact of increased creativity. As Abraham Maslow recognized in his celebrated study of psychologically healthy individuals – what he called self-actualized people – greater creativity is a hallmark of inner maturity. He concluded that: 'The concept of creativeness and the concept of the healthy, self-actualizing, fully human person seem to be coming closer and closer together, and may perhaps turn out to be the same thing.'

Creativity is a natural function of the human mind. It is something we are all blessed with. Where we differ is in the ways we use it – some may channel it into making music, some into cooking, some into making money, some into playing games – and the degree to which we express it. And the degree to which we express our creativity is a reflection of the boundaries we impose upon our thinking. These are the mindsets we have about what is possible and what is acceptable – and what our own creativity is capable of. If people were to grow increasingly liberated from these self-imposed limitations, human creativity would blossom as never before.

Furthermore, as our consciousness evolved, the directions in which we chose to direct this emergent creativity might also change. Less attached to the belief that we must change the world in order to find inner peace, we would not be so compelled to stoke the fires of material progress. We could begin to channel our creativity in more constructive directions. Into the furtherance of our conscious evolution. Into helping each other break free of the ties that bind us. Into improving the quality of our relationships, both with each other and with the other species that share this world. Into creating a new understanding of reality and our role within it.

Again we see positive feedback at work. The more free we were in ourselves, the more creative we would become. And the more creative we became, the better we could apply ourselves to the task of freeing ourselves.

In short, inner evolution would wind itself into ever-faster rates of change as surely as our material evolution has. The difference would be that our rate of inner evolution would be many times faster. As ever, our curve of development would be growing steeper and steeper.

Thus the idea of a rosy, stable 'new age' stretching hundreds, or even thousands, of years into the future seems most unlikely – at least for the foreseeable future.

A Blind Spot on the Future

Because we find it difficult to entertain an ever-growing pace of life, most of us have developed a blind spot on the future. We can imagine how things will be if they keep on changing as they are now – and even that can make us pretty dizzy – but we find it hard to picture a world in which change keeps coming faster and faster. As a result we overlook, or ignore, the full consequences of this trend.

Most future scenarios, whether made by corporate strategists, government think-tanks, or science fiction writers, generally assume that the pace of development will continue at a similar pace to today – or perhaps a little faster. Seldom do forecasters consider the impact of continued exponential acceleration.

In the early 1950s, for example, eminent scientists were predicting that it would take at least fifty years to put a person on the moon, primarily because it would take that long to make all the necessary technological advances. They underestimated the increased rates of progress that led to this goal being achieved in only fifteen years.

In the same way the growth of information technology has been consistently underestimated. The TV series 'Star Trek' was set to happen two hundred years in the future, by which time computers would no longer use magnetic tape, and would synthesize human speech. We may not yet have bravely trod beyond our own solar system, but as far as computers are concerned, reality caught up with fantasy in less than twenty years.

A study by Univac in 1950 concluded that five computers would meet the total world demand for the 'foreseeable future.'

A few years later a company by the name of International Business Machines took a look at the growing computer market, and decided it was too small to be worth getting into. Not long afterwards it ate its words, abbreviated its name, and caught up.

There is no reason to believe that we are not making similar mistakes in the present day. If we do survive these challenging times and move on in our evolution, then it seems more than probable that the pace of change will continue to quicken.

Time Compression

The implications of sustained acceleration are quite staggering. The amount of development that humanity has experienced in the two hundred years since the Industrial Revolution is similar to – possibly greater than – the amount of development that occurred over the preceding two thousand years. This in turn was of an order of magnitude similar to or greater than the changes of the previous twenty thousand years.

If rates of progress continue to speed up, we could see the same amount of development compressed into a few decades.

And then in mere years.

And after that . . . ?

Who knows, we could experience as many leaps in our own lifetimes as have occurred in the whole of evolution so far.

SPIRALS –
THE SHAPE OF THE FUTURE

Now there is more 'now' than there was even a few
months ago, and even more 'now' is on the way.

E.T. 101

So far we have considered evolution's acceleration as an ever-
steepening curve; but we might also consider it as an inward-
turning spiral in which each successive circuit is accomplished in a
shorter time.

Some spirals go on forever. If each circuit is a constant fraction –
one half, say – of the previous circuit, then however many circuits

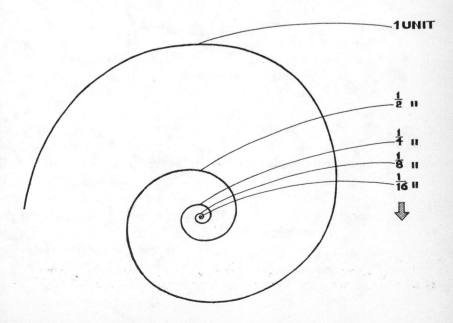

of the spiral you might make, there will always be more, yet smaller turns ahead. In fact there will always be an infinite number of turns ahead. You can continue going around and around the center without ever actually reaching it.

Paradoxically, although such spirals go on forever, they have a finite length. If the first circuit of the spiral were one unit long, the next circuit would be half a unit long, the next a quarter, then an eighth . . . and so on. The total length of the spiral would be $1+\frac{1}{2}+\frac{1}{4}+\frac{1}{8}+\frac{1}{16}+\frac{1}{32}+\frac{1}{64}+\frac{1}{128}\ldots$ units long. The series of numbers goes on indefinitely but its sum is finite. However many terms are added, the sum will get closer and closer to, but will never quite equal, two.

THE SHAPE OF EVOLUTION

When we look a little more closely at the evolutionary spiral that has led to the present time, we find that it appears to have followed a similar pattern – although not with such mathematical precision.

The creation of the Earth was preceded by approximately ten billion years of stellar evolution. The evolution of simple life forms took place over a couple of billion years. And multicellular life appeared a billion or so years ago. The evolution of complex nervous systems, made possible by the emergence of vertebrates, began several hundred million years ago. Mammals appeared tens of millions of years ago. A few million years ago the genus *Homo* first stood on the planet. Our own species, *Homo sapiens,* appeared several hundred thousand years ago. The shift to *Homo sapiens sapiens* that was triggered by the emergence of language and tool use, and that resulted in the Agricultural Revolution, began tens of thousands of years ago. The movement together into towns and cities started several thousand years ago. The Industrial Revolution began a few centuries ago. And the Information Revolution is but a few decades old.

Comparing successive stages we find that each new development occurred in about a tenth the time of the previous one. An exception occurred early on when multicellular organisms and the first verte-brates both took billions of years to emerge. Apart from that, each turn of the evolutionary spiral has been approximately a tenth the order of magnitude of the previous turn. This suggests that the spiral of evolu-

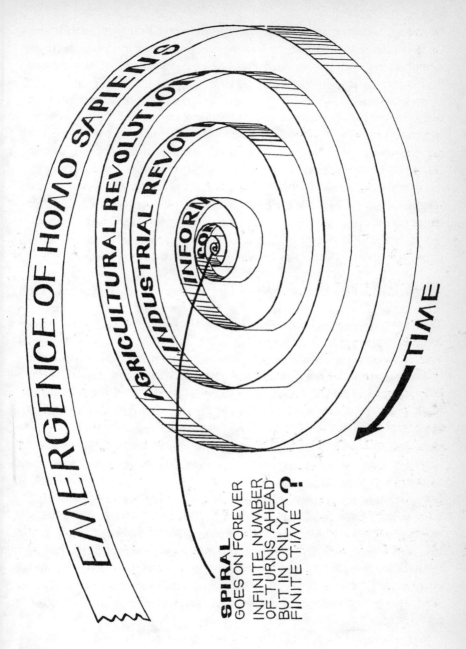

EMERGENCE OF HOMO SAPIENS

AGRICULTURAL REVOLUTION

INDUSTRIAL REVOL

INFORM

CO

TIME

SPIRAL
GOES ON FOREVER

INFINITE NUMBER
OF TURNS AHEAD
BUT IN ONLY A
FINITE TIME **?**

tion is of the same general type as the spiral we first considered.*

If evolution continues to follow this pattern, similar paradoxical conclusions will apply. Although there may be countless turns of the evolutionary spiral still ahead of us, the total length of the spiral could be finite. We could find ourselves evolving so fast that we completed our evolution within a finite time.

Timewave Zero

Similar conclusions have been arrived at by the American philosopher of science, Terence McKenna. His exploration starts with the ancient Chinese view of time. Noting some singular coincidences between old Chinese calendars and their 'Book of Changes,' *I Ching*, he derives a mathematical function which, he suggests, is a 'timewave' reflecting the overall rate of ingression of novelty into the world. The curve that results is not a smooth curve, but one that has peaks and troughs corresponding to the peaks and troughs of human history.**

The most significant characteristic of McKenna's timewave is that the shape repeats itself, but over shorter and shorter intervals of time. The curve shows a surge in novelty between 15000 and 8000 B.C. corresponding to the approximate dates of the Neolithic Age and the emergence of agriculture. Exactly the same pattern is repeated, although sixty-four times faster, from A.D.1750 to 1825 – the period known as the European Enlightenment and the beginning of the Industrial Era.

Another surge of novelty occurred around 500 B.C. This was the time when Lao Tsu, Plato, Zoroaster, Buddha, and others were having a major influence on the millennia to come. It saw the rise of Ancient Greece and the beginnings of European culture. This surge continued for several centuries, then slowed down in the fourth century A.D. with the Fall of Rome, and finally spluttered to an end with the onset of the Dark Ages. The repeating nature of McKen-

* One might feel that other significant events should be included in this list, or that some that have been included should be dropped. This would lead to different sets of times and to different ratios between them. Nevertheless, most such variations still result in spirals that are of the same general type – even though the turns may not be as evenly spaced as those above.

** A good summary of McKenna's ideas can be found in the journal *ReVISION*, vol. 10:1, Summer 1987.

na's timewave shows the same pattern recurring in the twentieth century, from 1967 through to the early 1990s – again sixty-four times as fast as before. Later, around 2010, it repeats again, and sixty-four times faster still.

This repeating historical pattern corresponds to a spiral in which each circuit is one sixty-fourth the length of the previous one. The curve goes on repeating itself an infinite number of times, but as with other spirals of this type its total length is finite. That is to say, it comes to a definite end – a time when the cycles of change are compressed from years to months to weeks to days. . . . McKenna calls this point 'Timewave Zero.' Its date, according to his calculations, is December 2012.*

The year 2012 seems frighteningly close. One's immediate response might be that rates of change could not become that fast in so short a time. Yet we should not forget that when estimating the pace of the future we tend to think in terms of today's pace, and our initial projections nearly always fall short. Many as yet unforeseen advances and revolutions could take the rate of change far beyond what we now imagine possible.

We should also remember that it would not be the material world that would be changing so fast, but our own inner world.

An Evolutionary Asymptote?

Needless to say, McKenna's formula is only one possible model of the curve of human history. Several other people interested in the future of our species have attempted to fit mathematical curves to our accelerating development. But the task is not easy and inevitably involves making a number of assumptions.

How, for example, do we measure 'progress'? Was the development of the atomic bomb a step of progress? Should one count social and political innovations such as the welfare state along with scientific discoveries and technological breakthroughs? And what values should be assigned to particular advances? Was the invention

---

* It is interesting to note that December 2012 also happens to be the last date in the calendar devised by the Mayan Indians. These people were obsessed with time and constructed a most elaborate calendar based on complex cycles of 4, 7, 9, 13, and 20. Why they chose this unusual structure is not clear, but whatever their reasons one fact is readily apparent: their calendar completes its 5,200 circle on December 22, 2012 – a fact that the American visionary Jose Arguelles and others have made much of.

of photocopying as significant as that of the printing press?

Even having chosen a set of significant steps and plotted them as a graph, it is still not easy to see what type of function describes the curve. There certainly are mathematical techniques for deciding how well an equation fits a curve. But having found a 'best fit,' the possibility always remains that some untried type of function might fit even better.

The result is a variety of graphs each approximating the pattern of human evolution, but none exact or definitive. Even so, most of them do have one tendency in common. Sooner or later they become asymptotic – that is to say, they approach the vertical. Some, such as McKenna's, place this asymptote in the near future, others put it a century or two ahead.

This suggests that if we do survive our present challenges, and if our evolution does continue to accelerate, we could see the whole of our future evolution – as much development as we can conceive of, and more – compressed into a century or so. Within a few generations, perhaps within our own lifetimes, we could reach the center of the spiral.

Within a finite time we could taste infinity.

Coping with Compression

There are, of course, many reasons why we may not reach the final stages of compression. First we have to steer our way through our current set of crises. And even if we do survive these challenges, we may well discover further testing points ahead. If we fail to respond to them appropriately we might find ourselves set back to some earlier, and slower, phase of evolution.

There is also the question of whether our minds could tolerate ever-increasing change. We might, for example, be able to cope with a pace double that of today, and possibly a pace ten times as fast. But what about a hundred times, or a thousand times? Is there an ultimate limit to how fast the human mind can adapt?

From our current mode of consciousness it may be very hard to imagine ourselves coping with such astronomical rates of change. But who knows what might be possible as our minds are liberated from their attachment to the material world. We may relate to change in a very different way; and our minds may then operate at a very different pace.

Something like this appears to happen at the point of death. Relieved of its ties to the senses, the mind seems to function at an altogether different speed. People who have brushed with death often report seeing the whole of their life flash before their eyes. In clock time the review may only last a second or so; but in that 'moment' they can relive years of experience.

Finally, we should recall that future turns of our evolutionary spiral are likely to be less material in nature. If we do come through these troubled times and go on with our development, it will be our perceptions, our attitudes, our thinking, and our awareness that will be changing faster and faster, not necessarily the world around. We will be experiencing an ever-accelerating spiral of inner awakening. This may turn out to be far easier to handle. Indeed, we might welcome it.

OMEGA –
A SINGULARITY IN TIME

The day will come when, after harnessing the winds, the
tides and gravitation, we shall harness for God the
energies of Love. And on that day, for the second time
in the history of the world, man will have discovered
fire.

Teilhard de Chardin

The acceleration of evolution towards a time of infinitely rapid
change is not so exceptional as one might at first suppose. The
evolution of matter in a star follows a similar pattern.

For 99.99 percent of its existence a star burns hydrogen, fusing
the atoms into helium and radiating the energy released as light.
Eventually the hydrogen runs out. For a star the size of our Sun this
happens after about 10,000 million years – it is currently about half
way through its life. Larger stars burn up more quickly, smaller
ones can last as long as 100,000 million years.

When all the hydrogen has been consumed a star can, if it is
massive enough, switch to burning the helium it has created,
transforming it into carbon. This keeps the star going for another
million years or so. When the helium is used up the star can survive
for another thousand years by fusing the carbon into neon. And
when the carbon runs out the star burns the neon to form silicon.
But the neon is exhausted within a year. Then, in a process that lasts
only a few days, the silicon fuses into iron.

That is as far as a star can go along this particular path. Fusing
iron does not release energy; it requires additional energy. The
star's fire begins to die – and with it the energy that until now has
supported the weight of its outer layers. Very quickly it begins to
collapse.

As its matter becomes increasingly compressed, its gravitational field increases. Within minutes it becomes so intense that even atoms cannot withstand the pressure. Electrons are stripped away and atomic nuclei pack in upon each other, reaching densities of more than a million tons per cubic inch. This disintegration releases enormous amounts of energy, blowing off the star's outer layers in what is known as a 'supernova.' This is one of the Universe's more spectacular shows. More energy is released during these few seconds than over the rest of the star's entire life.

Left behind is a neutron star – a solid mass of neutrons a mere fifteen or so miles across. For a sufficiently massive star (one about three times the mass of the Sun) the gravitational field becomes so strong that matter itself breaks down – and with it space and time. The star is said to have reached a singularity: a point at which the laws of physics no longer work. Mathematical equations become filled with zeros and infinities and cease to make any sense. There is a hole in space.

So intense is the gravitational field nothing can escape it. Even light is pulled back down. Nothing can be seen of the star. It has become a 'black hole.'

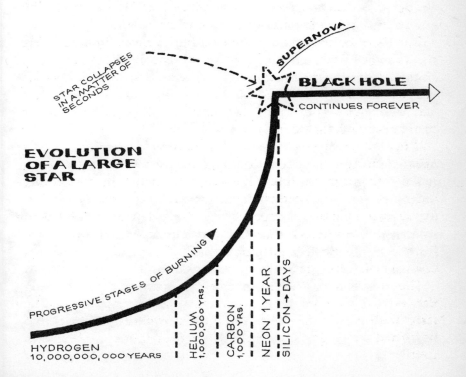

The Gravity of Love

The parallels between the evolution of a star and the pattern we have traced in the evolution of humanity are intriguing. Not only do both show an accelerating pattern of development; the factors behind this acceleration are analogous.

Whereas a star's matter is pulled together by the force of gravity, a species such as ourselves is pulled forward by our search for a more satisfying inner state. Our minds gravitate towards inner peace. We may not at first see this to be our goal. Caught up in our material desires we may believe it is comfort, security, or some other worldly satisfaction that we want. But the closer we draw to our own center, the clearer it becomes that, beneath everything, we are seeking inner peace and love. And the more we recognize our true goal, the faster we are able to move towards it.

In some respects gravity and love are not that different. Gravity is the attraction of mass for itself. It is a force that pulls the physical Universe back towards its original unity. Similarly, love can be considered as the attraction of life for itself – the desire for conscious union. Its ultimate expression is reunion with our own source, with the essence of our consciousness. It is this that is pulling us faster and faster along our evolutionary spiral towards a possible singularity in time. Buckminster Fuller summed it up poetically in his revised Lord's Prayer: 'Love,' he wrote, 'is metaphysical gravity.'

Horizons in Time

Another similarity between stellar evolution and our own conscious evolution concerns the 'event horizon' that surrounds a black hole. This is the region within which the gravitational force is so strong that not even light can escape. Since nothing can travel faster than light there is no way that any information can get out across this boundary. It is, in effect, an information horizon.*

A parallel horizon could well exist for humanity – except that this time it would be a horizon in time rather than one in space. A

---

* Stephen Hawking and others have shown that this may not be strictly true. Quantum effects may allow some energy and information to escape, but this need not concern us here. It does, however, suggest some further interesting parallels that you may, if you are so inclined, care to ponder.

ANATOMY OF
A BLACK HOLE

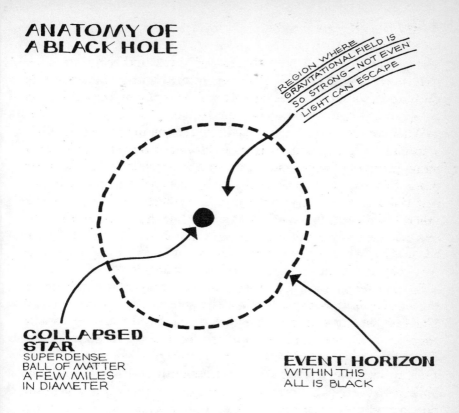

REGION WHERE GRAVITATIONAL FIELD IS SO STRONG – NOT EVEN LIGHT CAN ESCAPE

**COLLAPSED
STAR**
SUPERDENSE
BALL OF MATTER
A FEW MILES
IN DIAMETER

EVENT HORIZON
WITHIN THIS
ALL IS BLACK

thousand years ago change was much slower and the future a hundred years on would not have been markedly different. By the time of the Industrial Revolution the pace of life had increased dramatically making it much more difficult to foretell the future a hundred years ahead. But it would still have been possible to predict a decade or two into the future with reasonable certainty.

Today it is not possible to see even that far ahead. Unforeseen environmental changes have shown that we can no longer predict the future of the world more than a few years ahead. So closely are our affairs now interwoven that unexpected events in one person's mind can have reverberations around the world, changing the future for all concerned. And when economies crash without warning, the best-laid plans of machines and men can vanish overnight.

There is in effect an information horizon ahead of us – albeit a somewhat fuzzy one. Beyond this horizon the future will probably be nothing like we anticipate. And the faster change comes, the closer this horizon approaches.

As the predictable future shrinks from decades to years to months and less, there may well come a time when it is difficult to make any forecasts at all. We will have crossed our 'prediction horizon.'

History will have become chaotic – not chaotic in the sense of disorganized, but in the mathematical sense of unpredictable. However much progress we may have made in our inner evolution, we will not be able to be sure what is coming next. And it will be coming faster and faster. Completely unexpected developments could be always just around the corner.

The Value of Uncertainty

Having to face increasing uncertainty could play an important role in our inner liberation. As long as we are looking to the future for our fulfillment, uncertainty spells insecurity – and insecurity is something most of us find hard to handle. If we insist on holding on to our attachments, the changes we will encounter will probably drive us crazy. They will incline us more towards setback than breakthrough.

Only through letting go of our need for certainty, and our concern for how things might or might not be, will we find the inner stability to see us through such changeful times. In this regard increasing change may be just the trigger we need to shake us to our senses.

Again one might draw a parallel with the later stages of stellar evolution. In a collapsing star the ultra-intense gravitational field breaks down the very structure of matter, returning it to its fundamental constituents. With our own inner evolution it may take ultra-intense rates of change to bring about the breakdown of our materialism – of our belief that we need to get the world to be a certain way before we can be at peace. Increasing compression could be another challenge to accept the present moment.

The End of Evolution

So, where might evolution take us as we head towards the center of our spiral?

The great mystical traditions are unanimous in maintaining that liberation of the mind from its attachments, enlightening as it may be, is only the first of many steps of inner awakening. Beyond it are more universal experiences of mind, deeper understandings and richer perspectives of reality leading on to higher states of consciousness.

Is there a highest state of consciousness? Mahayana Buddhism talks of 'sahaj samadhi' – the recognition that *all* phenomena are merely consciousness in its various manifestations. Zen Buddhists speak of total non-duality. Hindu texts refer to the highest state of consciousness as unity with Brahman – a state in which one knows the source of all creation and all its levels of manifestation. And Christian mystics talk of 'oneness with God.'

Whether or not these descriptions are referring to exactly the same state of consciousness is a question I shall leave to those more qualified than me. Nevertheless they would all seem to be pointing in the same direction – towards a personal evolutionary zenith.

So what might happen, one might ask, if this were to become a collective experience rather than a blessing bestowed upon one in a hundred million? Would our collective evolution then come to an end? Could it be that, in much the same way as the destiny of matter in a sufficiently massive star is to become a black hole in space, the destiny of a self-conscious species – should it be sufficiently full of love – is a 'spiritual supernova.' Is this what we are accelerating towards? A moment when the light of inner awakening radiates throughout the world? A white hole in time?

Omega Point

One person who believed this was indeed our destiny was the French priest and paleontologist, Pierre Teilhard de Chardin, who lived in the first half of this century. Exploring the evolutionary trends towards greater complexity, connectivity, and consciousness, he argued that humanity was moving towards an 'Omega Point' – the full descent of spirit into matter, the fulfillment of our evolution. In the concluding words of his essay *My Universe* he writes:

Like a vast tide, Being will have engulfed the shifting sands of being. Within a now tranquil ocean, each drop of which, nevertheless, will be conscious of remaining itself, the astonishing adventure of the world will have ended. The dream of every mystic, the eternal pantheist ideal, will have found its full and legitimate satisfaction.

Where Teilhard de Chardin's picture differs from that presented here is in the time-scales involved. He saw this peak of human evolution to be a long way off – millions of years in the future. But, like many others before and after, he did not take the implications of an ever-accelerating pace of development into full account. Had he done so he might have arrived at a very much earlier date.

Teilhard de Chardin described the Omega Point as a time when light would blaze across the planet – not physical light but the light of consciousness. Like a mirror polished to give a perfect reflection of the Sun, all those apparently separate rays of consciousness peering through a billion holes in the fabric of time and space would know themselves to be the same eternal light – the light behind all creation.

The End of Time

Then, at last, our evolution's ever-accelerating trend would come to an end. We would have reached the center of our spiral.

But this would not, it must be emphasized, signify an end to the world – well at least not in the sense that we normally mean it. It would certainly mean an end to our attachment to the world. An end to our dysfunctional attitudes and behavior. An end to the world as we know it now.

It would also be an end to our attachment to time. We would know ourselves to be in essence Mind, outside of time. But time itself would not end. Our bodies would live on. And so would the species. We would be free, at last, to truly enjoy our world. And might continue that way for a very long – much as the dolphins and whales have before us.

But there is a sense in which this full awakening might be an end. And that is in the sense of purpose. Could there be an evolutionary summit towards which Creation has been building since time began? Could there in this sense be an 'end' to Creation?

Surprisingly – or perhaps not – this is a question that physics has now begun to ponder.

PURPOSE –
A DESIGN TO CREATION?

'Any coincidence,' said Miss Marple to herself, 'is always worth noting. You can throw it away later if it is only a coincidence.'

Agatha Christie

Purpose is not something physics usually concerns itself with. It sees the Universe unfolding according to a pre-ordained set of laws. We may not understand all the laws, and even when we do we may not be able to predict exactly how things will behave – as quantum physics and chaos theory have both made clear. None the less, being laws they leave no room for purpose. At least, not in the sense of striving towards a goal.

However, this is not the only sense in which things can have a purpose. There can also be purpose in design. A clock runs according to well-defined physical laws – what value would there be in one that didn't? But this does not mean it has no purpose. It was constructed and set running in such a way that its movements would have meaning. The question that some scientists are now beginning to ask is: Could the same be true of the Universe? Could it run according to the laws of physics, yet be set up to run in a particular direction?

A Coincidental Universe?

You might think that more or less any Universe is possible. Of course, not all Universes would be the same – changing some of Nature's fundamental constants might lead to different physical laws and to Universes that behaved in ways quite unlike our own – but they would still exist. However, it is now being realized that this may not be the case. It appears that if the conditions of the original creation were not exactly as they were the Universe would simply not have worked.

Physicists believe that at the time of the Big Bang the number of particles created was very slightly greater than the number of anti-particles – about one part in a billion more. Whenever particles and anti-particles meet they annihilate each other; and within a short time of the Big Bang all the anti-particles had met their match and disappeared – along with a corresponding number of particles. But because of the initial inequality some matter remained. This matter became the Universe we know. Had it not been for this initial imbalance, there would have been no galaxies, no stars, no planets, nor even the simplest of chemical elements.

Moreover the total number of matter particles left over – about 10^{80} (1 followed by 80 zeros) – was also critical. If the number had been a little greater the gravitational forces would have been stronger than the energy of expansion. The young Universe would have rapidly collapsed in upon itself to form one huge black hole.

Conversely, if the number had not been quite so large, gravitational forces would have been weaker, and the Universe would have expanded so rapidly that galaxies would never have had time to form. Again, the Universe as we know it would not have existed.

Another factor crucial for the existence of matter was the mass of the neutron – the particle that together with the proton forms atomic nuclei. If this were only 0.2 percent less than its actual value, protons would have rapidly decayed into neutrons and no atoms would ever have been formed.

The atoms that initially formed were those of hydrogen. However, before these could evolve into the second element, helium, there had to be some other 'lucky' coincidences. If the nuclear force, which holds atomic nuclei together against their electromagnetic repulsion, were a few percent weaker, deuterium – a stage that hydrogen passes through as it combines to form helium – would have been very unstable. The Universe would have remained almost pure hydrogen.

If, on the other hand, the nuclear forces had been a few percent stronger all the hydrogen in the Universe would have burnt to helium in a matter of seconds. And with all the hydrogen gone there would have been no fuel for stars.

Before helium could evolve into other elements, such as carbon, oxygen, and nitrogen, another coincidence was necessary. The charge on the proton had to be just right. If it had been slightly larger the nuclei of these heavier atoms would not have been stable. They would have decayed rapidly leaving a Universe of only hydrogen and helium.

The further evolution of matter into elements heavier than iron had to wait for the first stars to complete their life cycle and turn into supernova, which released the additional energy that was needed for the synthesis of these larger atoms. But the fact that stars can reach this stage at all depends upon some other fine tunings. If the force of gravity were very slightly stronger, the electromagnetic force very slightly weaker, or the electron slightly less heavy, the convective processes within stars would have been very different. Most stars would have been unable to evolve beyond the stage of burning helium. They would never have reached the stage of supernova. And without supernova there would have been no heavy elements, and no possibility for life.

The Coincidence of Life

However, before life could begin, some other very fine tunings were necessary.

Life as we know it is based upon carbon. All the proteins, amino acids, vitamins, fats, and carbohydrates which make up your body are molecules built on a skeleton of carbon. It was once thought that life based on silicon, or even some other element, might also be possible; but it is now generally believed that only carbon offers the variety and complexity of bonds that living systems depend upon. Yet the very existence of carbon rests on a most precise and unusual coincidence.

Carbon atoms are synthesized in stars by the fusion of three helium atoms. Very rarely do three atoms meet at exactly the same time. Instead two helium nuclei first combine to the nucleus of beryllium atom. But this nucleus is unstable, and would decay before it had much chance of capturing a third helium nucleus – were it not for a very lucky coincidence. Because of a phenomenon called nuclear resonance, a beryllium nucleus can capture helium nuclei from a much larger surrounding area. This greatly increases its chances of combining with a third helium atom to form carbon.

If the nuclear resonance level for carbon were not exactly the value it is, virtually no carbon would have formed inside stars, and life would never have existed.

However, this is only half the story. A fourth helium nucleus will combine with the carbon atom to form oxygen. If this reaction were also 'resonant' – that is, if carbon could capture helium from a wider area – carbon itself would have rapidly 'burnt' and disappeared. Curiously, the nuclear resonance for oxygen lies just below the critical value.

Not only are these two resonances a most remarkable pair of coincidences, they are themselves the result of some very fine tuning between the strengths of nuclear and electromagnetic interactions, along with the relative masses of electrons and protons.

The Water of Life

Another set of coincidences thought to be essential for the evolution of any life form relates to the unusual properties of water. Water may seem very ordinary, but it is one of the strangest substances known to science. Its solid state, ice, is lighter than its liquid state – a virtually unique property. If ice did not float on water, it would sink to the ocean floor where it would accumulate, gradually freezing the seas from the bottom up.

The fact that ice stays on the surface has another advantage. It protects creatures in the water from the extremes of temperature above. Were it not for this most unusual property it is doubtful that life in the oceans could have evolved very far at all.

Water has an unusually high specific heat; that is, it can absorb large amounts of heat with only a relatively small rise in temperature. This, together with its high thermal conductivity, gives water a stabilizing effect on the environment. It also has a higher surface tension than any other substance except liquid selenium. Not only does this allow insects to skate across its surface; more importantly it tends to concentrate organic molecules at the surface of the liquid, speeding up biochemical reactions considerably.

These and several other very unusual properties of water arise from its particular molecular shape, and the strength of the forces holding it together. These are in turn consequences of other very delicate tunings of Nature's fundamental constants. Were it not for these coincidences, and these anomalous properties of water, it is very unlikely that life would ever have evolved as far as simple cells.

Nor does water stand alone. Oxygen and nitrogen, two principal elements of organic chemistry, also possess very special properties that make them ideally suited to evolution.

And the list goes on.

The deeper one looks, the more it appears that the initial conditions of the cosmos, the strength of the 'bang,' and the values of nature's fundamental constants were precisely those required to produce a physical Universe that was stable, that would evolve into a diversity of chemical elements and eventually be able to sustain life.

The Anthropic Principle

How does one make sense of this remarkable collection of coincidences? Has some super-intelligence been at work adjusting the laws of physics in order to create the Universe the way it is? Or are they all just coincidences – however remarkable?

Scientists' attempts to answer such questions have given rise to what is known as 'The Anthropic Principle.' In its most general form this states that the only Universe that can contain human beings (*anthropos* in Greek) – and hence the only Universe that we can observe – is one in which these coincidences are exactly as they are. If they were not, we would not be here to notice the fact.

It may sound simple, but the principle is open to some radically differing interpretations. What is known as the 'Weak Anthropic Principle' falls very much in line with the conventional scientific paradigm, which excludes any notion of a 'grand design' – let alone any 'Grand Old Designer.' It proposes that our very existence as human beings determines the type of Universe we can observe. It is not so much an accident that all the parameters are exactly as they are; it is an inevitability. We cannot possibly know of any other types of Universe, for we would not be around to observe them.

Some proponents of this view hold that there may in fact be numerous other Universes existing in parallel with our own. Others suggest there have been numerous Universes preceding ours and that numerous others are yet to follow. In each of these other Universes the fundamental constants might well be different. Only in a minute fraction of them – probably less than one in a billion – would the conditions be right for life to evolve. All others would be devoid of life, devoid of intelligent observers, and thus forever unknowable.

This, however, raises the question of whether or not an unknowable Universe can be said to exist.

In an attempt to deal with this philosophical problem, and also to handle some of the stranger coincidences that are harder to explain by the Weak Anthropic Principle, cosmologists such as Fred Hoyle in England and John Wheeler in the U.S.A. have developed an alternative 'Strong Anthropic Principle.' They argue that there can be no matter without an observer, for only when you make an observation do you convert the probability functions of quantum mechanics into actualities. Thus the only Universes that can exist are those that can be observed.

This implies that the initial conditions of any Universe *must be* such as to allow that Universe to exist . . . to exist long enough for life to emerge . . . and for that life to be able to evolve into beings capable of observing the Universe. In other words, the Universe exists so that it can be known.

KNOWING –
THE ENDS OF THE UNIVERSE

From joy all beings are born
By joy they are all sustained,
And into joy they again return.

Taittiriya Upanishad

The gathering and processing of information has been one of evolution's principal threads. The first breakthrough was DNA, which gave matter the ability to store and reproduce information, and became the molecular data bank of Life. Later, sexual reproduction allowed two organisms to share their genetic learnings, speeding up a thousandfold the rate at which Life's growing body of data could be processed and built upon.

As living systems evolved they learned to detect changes in their environment – changes in chemistry, heat, light, pressure, and vibration. Life had began to sense the world around.

Nervous systems evolved to process this sensory data and turn it into useful information. Incoming information from several different senses could be integrated into a coherent model of the world. Experiences could be remembered and drawn upon at later times.

The nervous systems of some creatures became so large they were able to perform the very complex information processing necessary for symbolic language. Such creatures could share their learnings with each other, and think about the world they saw. They began to form concepts, establish general principles, and so construct a picture of the world in which they found themselves. Nature had begun to know itself.

Thus began our quest for meaning. We became hungry for knowledge, asking no end of questions in our search for understanding. We even thought about the very process of knowing; and to ensure our knowledge was reliable, we organized our quest into disciplines of science.

Our ability to mold the world into new forms led to tools and technologies that added to our powers of knowing. No longer did we have to rely only upon our own senses. We created electron microscopes, radio telescopes, X-ray cameras, mass spectrometers, and bubble chambers. We peered into the depths of matter and out into the further reaches of space. How did the Universe come to be? How does it function? Where is it going?

Now, after millennia of seeking, we seem to be closing in on some of the answers. We can look out to the edges of the Universe, back to times when the first galaxies were forming; we can begin to understand how it all started and how it has developed. We have looked back over the history of Life on Earth and put together a picture of how we came to be. We have discovered the molecular code in the genes and are piecing together the hundred million instructions of our own biological program. We have realized that space and time are manifestations of a deeper underlying continuum; and that matter and energy are similarly related. And we seem, at last, to be approaching a unified field theory – an integrated understanding of all the fundamental forces of nature in a single set of mathematical equations.

Needless to say, there is still much that we do not know. And much of what we do know may later prove only an approximation to the truth. But given how much knowledge we have gathered in just a few centuries – particularly in the last few decades – it seems unlikely that it will be another million years before our knowing is complete. Cross-fertilization and positive feedback will ensure our rate of progress in this direction continues to accelerate. We could learn as much in the next fifty years as in the last five thousand.

Inner Knowing

The Strong Anthropic Principle suggests that the Universe has to be one that can come to know itself. If so, it is unlikely that this knowing would be restricted to its physical manifestations. There is the equally real – in some respects more real – realm of Mind also waiting to be known.

As self-conscious entities we can take that inner step. We are aware of our thoughts and feelings. We are conscious of our knowledge; and conscious to some extent of the Self that knows. However, compared to our understanding of the world around, our knowledge of this inner realm is at present much more thinly spread.

We do know that more is possible. Dotted through history there have been those who have awakened to this inner realm in all its glory. They have come to know the essence of consciousness, and in doing so have realized that this inner essence is the essence of all creation. In the language of Indian philosophy, they have come to know that 'Atman,' the consciousness that manifests within us all, is 'Brahman,' the source of all Creation.

The vast majority of us may still be far from such realization. But it is the direction we are headed in, both as individuals and as a species. And, as we have seen, there are good reasons to believe that our inner awakening need not take a lot of time. We could, if we put our minds to it, find ourselves fulfilling this inner quest within a century or two – or even less.

Through us the source of Creation would then have come to know itself in all its dimensions. It would have come to know its physical manifestation in all its depth and beauty. It would have come to know its many levels of mental manifestations; and come to know the Self that lies behind them all. Its long journey of data gathering, information processing, knowing, and understanding would be complete. Through us the Universe would have accomplished its design.

A Universe of Knowing

This is not to imply that the fulfillment of this function rests with human beings alone. As far as we know, there is nothing unique about planet Earth. If the conditions here are right for life, they are almost certainly right on many other planets – a quadrillion according to the most optimistic estimates. Moreover, the fact that life on Earth got started soon after conditions here were right suggests that life probably takes hold wherever it can. The Universe could be teeming with life.

Moreover, the Strong Anthropic Principle postulates that the Universe not only has to permit the emergence of life, it must also permit the evolution of observers. If so, the Universe may be teeming with intelligence as well. There may be billions – perhaps quadrillions – of other self-conscious species out there, each in their own ways exploring the worlds around them and within them. Each in their own way rediscovering both the fullness and the essence of Creation. Each and every one of them an opportunity for cosmic self-discovery.

They may not all be at the same stage as us. Life on many planets may still be at the equivalent of bacteria or simple sponges. On many it may have passed our phase long ago. But there are very likely to be other planets, spread across the Universe, where evolution has reached a similar stage to that on Earth. There may be quite a few in our own galaxy.

From this perspective we are not, after all, that significant. No more than a single bud in a rose garden.

From the perspective of planet Earth, however, we are most significant. After billions of years a creature has arisen that has transcended biological evolution and entered the realm of ideas. It is our minds, not our bodies, that are evolving. And our minds are evolving together. We are a species that can explore and study its world. A species that looks for meaning. We are a species with self-consciousness; a species that knows that it knows. We can know the breadth of time; we can look back at where we have come from, and forward to where we might be going. And we can know our own intrinsic timelessness.

We may be the most creative, most intelligent, and most thoughtful creature the Earth has ever seen. And we have the potential to be much much more.

Could we be the moment Life's been waiting for? Could this be the meaning of our existence? Is there an end to our struggle?

Only time will tell.

THE END – OR THE BEGINNING?

Today is the first day of the rest of your life.

Abbie Hoffman

Whether or not this particular species on planet Earth will be able to blossom into full knowing is still an open question. We are an evolutionary seed cast into the winds of space-time. Whether or not we become all that we may be is up to us. We have been given every opportunity and facility. But we have also been given mastery of our own destiny.

We are, in effect, facing an evolutionary exam – a cosmic intelligence test. We have prodigious powers at our disposal – enough to harm a planet – and before we can continue our evolutionary journey we must prove that we have the wisdom to be the master of ourselves and thus use our creativity in ways that are beneficial to all.

This trial may not be unique to humankind on planet Earth. Any intelligent tool-using life form will probably meet a similar test. A species that can modify its environment is likely to use its creativity to improve its chances of survival. Doubtless it would be delighted with a longer life expectancy, and might not, at first, see any need to curb its biological productivity. Slowly, to begin with, its population would begin to grow.

So also would its technological abilities. As with any other evolutionary process, each new advance would facilitate further advances. Its rate of development would accelerate, and if it were not careful it might well find itself changing its world faster than its planetary biosystem could adjust.

Whether such a species would fall into the trap of egocentricity is an open question. If it did not, it might easily develop the wisdom and the will to manage its growing powers and so avoid catastrophe. But any technological species whose psychological development followed a similar course to ours would probably find themselves facing a parallel crisis of consciousness. If they were to survive, then they too would need to transcend self-centeredness.

To put it another way, any intelligent tool-using species enters a window in time. The window opens with the emergence of self-consciousness. The species then embarks upon a dash through history. Can its inner evolution keep pace with its material development? Can it make it through to a full awakening of the spirit before the side effects of misguided creativity force the window closed?

The window in time that opened when life on Earth took the leap into *Homo sapiens sapiens* is at the point of closing. We are in the last moments of our 50,000-year dash from emerging consciousness to full enlightenment. We are in a race against time itself.

It is we alive today who have the responsibility of guiding this species on. It is we who have to find ways to release ourselves from this self-centered phase of our development and open ourselves to the full significance of the timeless moment — and to the full significance of the present time.

We do indeed live in interesting times. Possibly the most interesting this planet has ever known.

The first day of the last month of the first year
of the last decade
of the last century of a millennium.

Mount Washington summit,
Full Moon at its north node and closest approach to Earth,
the largest and most brilliant of Moons,
Mars alongside, also at its brightest,
a trail of flight cleaving the two,
Capricorn guarding, lives changing,
governments talking of war,
business talking of new paradigms,
old enemies connecting, shaking hands beneath the sea,
temporally synchronistic sandwiches playing through our lives,
the end of a journey,
the end of the workbook,
thankful for many blessings,
at peace for a while,
wondering whether we can all be friends,
remembering the real work
and the choice we each must make,
– remembering not to worry.

ACKNOWLEDGMENTS

Many thanks go to many people. I will not detail what they have each contributed. That they each know. But I do wish to acknowledge how valuable their help has been – without any one of them this book would not be what it is – and how much I have appreciated their gifts. They are: Ian Farquhar, Marilyn Ferguson, Oliver Markeley, Marion Russell, Paul Wheeler, Judith Meynell, Lindsay Cooke, Cynthia Alves, Brian Weller (he did the illustrations), Ruth Strasberg, Ray Gottlieb, Shayla Spencer, Roger Evans, Bryn Jones, Leah Landau, Jane Henry, David Wynne, Bill Whitson, John Reilly, Tessa Strickland, Chris Hall, Juliet Weston-Lewis, Sheila Cane, Hag, Chris Coverdale, James Fraser, Rupert Sheldrake, Edward Posey, Kindred Gottlieb, Joe Sohm, Robert Taylor, Christopher Bowers, Sheila McCleod, Alexander Shulgun, Sylvia Timbers, Wendy Feldman, Roger Doudna, Pat Markeley, Terence McKenna, Ella Fallgren, Linda Hope, Mike Duguay, Willis Harman, Jan Bakelin, Gisela Pauli, Michael Toms, Mark Salzwedel, Eileen Campbell, Anne McDermid, and last, but in no sense least, Anna Pauli.

Five years is a long time to be working on a book, and there may be others whom I would wish to acknowledge had they not temporarily slipped my memory. If so please remind me. I won't be offended; and I trust you won't be either.

I would also like to thank Oxford University Press for permission to use the lines on page 165 from Christopher Fry's play *A Sleep of Prisoners* and Harper and Row for permission to quote the Rilke poem on page 11 translated by Stephen Mitchell from his book *The Enlightened Heart*.

INDEX